HARCOURT

Math

Challenge Workbook

TEACHER EDITION
Grade 3

Harcourt

Orlando   Austin   Chicago   New York   Toronto   London   San Diego

Visit *The Learning Site!*
www.harcourtschool.com

REPRODUCING COPIES FOR STUDENTS

This Teacher's Edition contains full-size student pages with answers printed in non-reproducible blue ink.

It may be necessary to adjust the exposure control on your photocopy machine to a lighter setting to ensure that blue answers do not reproduce.

Printed in the United States of America

ISBN 0-15-336517-X

4 5 6 7 8 9 10 054 10 09 08 07 06 05

CONTENTS

Name _____

Fact Family Search

Find the fact family in each square.
The number above each square is the greatest number in
the fact family.
You will find facts across and down. Not all numbers are
a part of each fact family.
Write +, −, and = signs between the numbers.
The first one has been done for you.

12

6	8 + 4 = 12
	+ −
12 − 4 = 8	8
	= =
6	4	12	4
8	12	10	2

17

8	17 − 8 = 9
+	+
9	10	7	8
=	=
17 − 9 = 8	17
8	7	15	9

14

5	9	5	4
	+	+	
14 − 5 = 9	5
−	=	=
9	14	14	9
=			
5	7	7	4

13

6	13	7	3
−			
7	6 + 7 = 13
+	=	−
6	7	10	7
=		=
13	7	3	6

16

7	7 + 9 = 16
	−
9	16	6	10
+	−	
7	9	7	4
=	=	
16 − 7 = 9	6

15

15	7	7	15
−			−
7 + 8 = 15	8
=		=
8 + 7 = 15	7
5	10	8	1

Make up your own fact family search. Give it to another
student to solve.

Name _____

Missing Addend Riddle

What kind of mouse never eats cheese?

Find the missing addends.

1. 5 + __7__ = 12 **E**	2. __2__ + 8 = 10 **P**
3. 9 + __6__ = 15 **A**	4. 1 + __15__ = 16 **T**
5. __9__ + 9 = 18 **M**	6. 8 + __4__ = 12 **S**
7. 9 + __1__ = 10 **R**	8. __10__ + 5 = 15 **C**
9. __5__ + 8 = 13 **O**	10. __8__ + 9 = 17 **M**
11. __16__ + 1 = 17 **U**	12. 0 + __14__ = 14 **O**
13. __3__ + 9 = 12 **U**	14. __0__ + 9 = 9 **E**

Use the addition problems above to solve the riddle.
Write the letter on the line that matches the addend
below the line.

A   C   O   M   P   U   T   E   R
6   10   14   9   2   3   15   7   1

M   O   U   S   E
8   5   16   4   0

CW2   **Challenge**

Colorful Matches

For each sum or set of addends in Column A, find a sum or set of addends in Column B that represents the same number. Then find a sum or set of addends in Column C that represents the same number.

Draw colored lines to connect the matching sums and addends.
- Draw a red line if the sum and addends show the Order Property of Addition.
- Draw a blue line if the sum and addends show the Identity Property of Addition.
- Draw a green line if the sum and addends show the Grouping Property of Addition.

The first one has been started for you. Trace the lines with the correct color.   Red ——— Blue ——— Green -----

Column A	Column B	Column C
9 + 3	11	0 + 16
16 + 0	0 + 9	8 + 9
(2 + 3) + 6	9 + 8	10
14	7 + (3 + 8)	9 + 0
4 + (7 + 4)	12	(7 + 3) + 8
9	16	2 + (3 + 6)
(2 + 8) + 3	8 + 2	13
17	5 + 9	15
2 + 8	(4 + 7) + 4	3 + 9
18	2 + (8 + 3)	9 + 5

Name _____

Addition Squares

Fill in the empty squares by adding the numbers across each row, and adding the numbers down each column.

1. (+)

83	7	90
9	64	73
92	71	163

2. (+)

46	34	80
31	6	37
77	40	117

3. (+)

25	42	67
39	48	87
64	90	154

4. (+)

65	27	92
30	25	55
95	52	147

5. (+)

46	18	64
25	62	87
71	80	151

6. (+)

39	39	78
53	12	65
92	51	143

7. (+) (+)

23	16	44	83
37	7	15	59
15	4	26	45
75	27	85	187

8. (+) (+)

9	31	56	96
12	6	17	35
41	23	4	68
62	60	77	199

CW4 **Challenge**

Subtraction Path

Find each difference. Then color each footprint with differences in the 40s.
Find the path from Start to Finish.

START

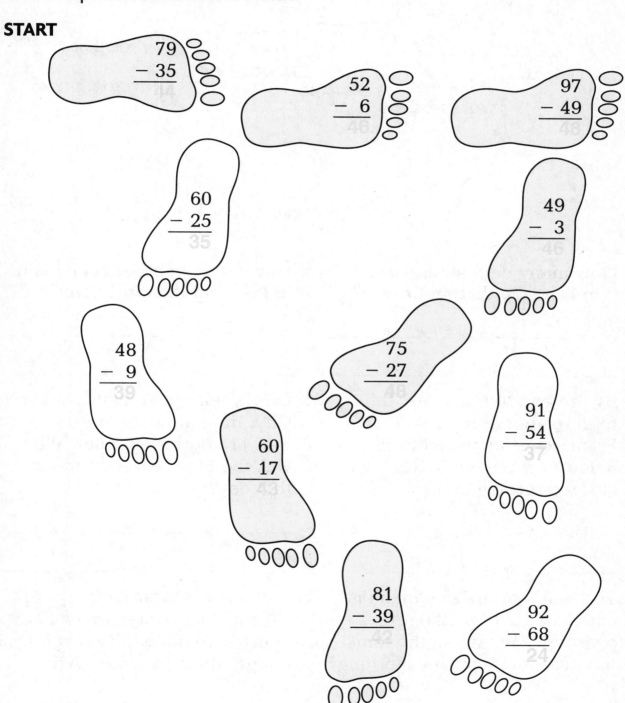

$$79 - 35 = 44$$

$$52 - 6 = 46$$

$$97 - 49 = 48$$

$$60 - 25 = 35$$

$$49 - 3 = 46$$

$$48 - 9 = 39$$

$$75 - 27 = 48$$

$$91 - 54 = 37$$

$$60 - 17 = 43$$

$$81 - 39 = 42$$

$$92 - 68 = 24$$

FINISH

Solving Problems Using a Weather Map

Use the map to solve the problems below. Tell what operation you used to solve each problem.

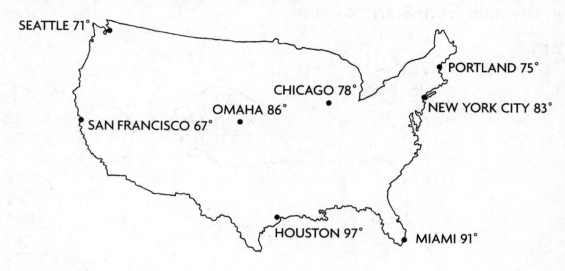

SEATTLE 71°

PORTLAND 75°

CHICAGO 78°

OMAHA 86°

NEW YORK CITY 83°

SAN FRANCISCO 67°

HOUSTON 97°

MIAMI 91°

1. How many degrees warmer is it in Houston than in Seattle?

_____ 26 degrees _____

_____ subtraction _____

2. How many degrees cooler is it in Portland than in Miami?

_____ 16 degrees _____

_____ subtraction _____

3. By the end of the week, the high temperature in San Francisco is expected to rise 8 degrees. What will the temperature be then?

_____ 75 degrees _____

_____ addition _____

4. One week ago in New York City, the high temperature was 11 degrees warmer. What was the high temperature on that day?

_____ 94 degrees _____

_____ addition _____

5. The temperature in Omaha is expected to drop 18 degrees overnight. What will the temperature be tomorrow morning?

_____ 68 degrees _____

_____ subtraction _____

6. Tomorrow's forecast for Chicago is an increase of 12 degrees. What will Chicago's temperature be tomorrow?

_____ 90 degrees _____

_____ addition _____

Odd-and-Even Game

Play with a partner.

Materials:

• Number chart shown below

• Number cube with numbers 1–6

• 30 game markers (15 each of two colors)

How to Play:

The object of the game is to get 5 of your markers in a row in any direction—horizontal, vertical, or diagonal.

Take turns. Roll the number cube. If the number is even, place a marker on any even number on the number chart. If the number is odd, place a marker on any odd number on the number chart.

1	2	3	4	5	6	7	8	9	10
11	12	13	14	15	16	17	18	19	20
21	22	23	24	25	26	27	28	29	30
31	32	33	34	35	36	37	38	39	40
41	42	43	44	45	46	47	48	49	50

Name _____

Colorful Balloons

Read the clues. Color the balloons.

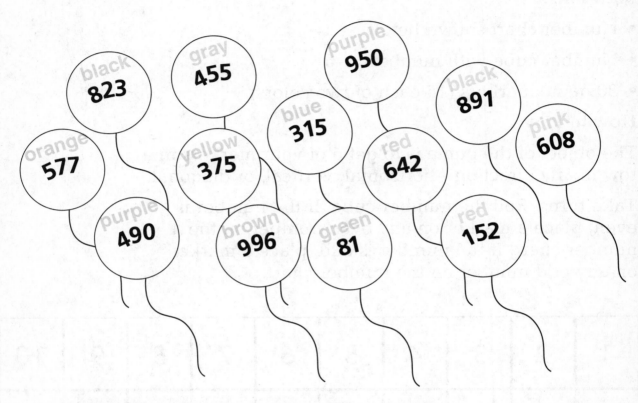

1. A balloon with a two in the ones place is red.

2. If the balloon has a one in the tens place, color it blue.

3. A balloon whose number equals 175 + 200 is yellow.

4. The balloon with the least number is green.

5. Color any balloon with a zero in the ones place purple.

6. The balloon with the greatest number is brown.

7. Any balloon whose number is 576 + 1 is orange.

8. A balloon with an eight in the hundreds place is black.

9. If the balloon has a zero in the tens place, color it pink.

10. If the number is 555 − 100, color the balloon gray.

CW8   Challenge

Arrays of Stars

Each sheet of stickers contains 1,000 stars. The stars are arranged in 50 rows with 20 stickers in each row. Use this information to answer each question.

1. A package of stickers contains 5,000 stars. How many sheets of stars are there?

_____5 sheets_____

2. Each teacher at Lakota Elementary received 9 sheets of stars. How many stars did each receive?

_____9,000 stars_____

3. If each sheet of stickers costs 50¢, how much would 12,000 stars cost?

_____$6_____

4. Mr. Lee used 3,894 stickers during the first grading period. How many sheets was this?

_____4 sheets_____

5. Mrs. Winslow used 2 sheets of stickers during the first grading period, 3 sheets during the second grading period and half of a sheet during the first week of the third grading period. How many stars did she use?

_____5,500 stars_____

6. Carrie used 8 rows of stars to decorate thank-you notes for the parents that helped on the last field trip. How many stars did she use?

_____160 stars_____

7. Martin made a design with the stars. He used one sheet of stars in the first row of his design, two sheets in the next row, three sheets in the third row, and so on. If his design had 6 rows, how many stars did he use?

_____21,000 stars_____

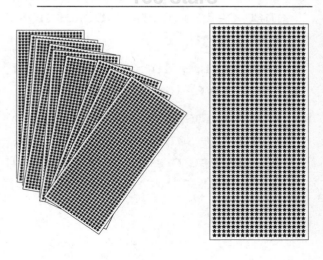

Problem Solving Strategy
Use Logical Reasoning

Read the clues. Color the squares on the hundred chart.

1	2	3	4	5	6	7	8	9	10
11	12	13	14	15	16	17	18	19	20
21	22	23	24	25	26	27	28	29	30
31	32	33	34	35	36	37	38	39	40
41	42	43	44	45	46	47	48	49	50
51	52	53	54	55	56	57	58	59	60
61	62	63	64	65	66	67	68	69	70
71	72	73	74	75	76	77	78	79	80
81	82	83	84	85	86	87	88	89	90
91	92	93	94	95	96	97	98	99	100

1. A 2-digit number the sum of whose digits is 1. 10

2. The last number on the hundred chart. 100

3. The number that is 99 less than the greatest number on the hundred chart. 1

4. Both digits are odd. The tens digit minus the ones digit is 4. Their sum is 10. 73

5. The digits are equal. The sum of the digits is 10. 55

6. The number that is 1 less than the number whose digits have a sum of 12 and whose tens digit is greater than 4 but less than 6. 56

7. The number whose digits have a sum of 15 and a difference of 1. This number is not 8 less than 95. 78

8. If you subtract 6 from the ones digit, you get the tens digit. Skip-count by 2 four times to get the ones digit. 28

9. The number that is 5 less than the answer to Problem 8. 23

10. The number whose ones digit is 8 less than its tens digit. The sum of the digits is a 2-digit number. 91

11. The number whose digits have a sum the same as the digits in 36. This number is less than 50 and greater than 36. 45

12. The number in the sixth column, fifth row. 46

Pattern Plans

Predict the next three numbers in each pattern.
Describe the pattern.

1. 957, 947, 937, 927, __917__, __907__, __897__

   Pattern: _____numbers decrease by 10_____

2. 132, 137, 142, 147, __152__, __157__, __162__

   Pattern: _____numbers increase by 5_____

3. 824, 821, 818, 815, __812__, __809__, __806__

   Pattern: _____numbers decrease by 3_____

4. 356, 360, 364, 368, __372__, __376__, __380__

   Pattern: _____numbers increase by 4_____

5. 640, 638, 636, 634, __632__, __630__, __628__

   Pattern: _____numbers decrease by 2_____

Make your own patterns by increasing or decreasing
3-digit numbers. Describe each pattern.

Patterns will vary. Check students' work.

6. _____, _____, _____, _____, _____, _____, _____

   Pattern: _____

   _____

7. _____, _____, _____, _____, _____, _____, _____

   Pattern: _____

   _____

Challenge CW11

Name _____

Matching Numbers

Match the correct standard form to the word form of the number.

1. eighty-three thousand,
   nine hundred seventy-six

2. ninety-four thousand,
   three hundred four

3. four hundred sixty-two thousand,
   five hundred ten

4. seventy-five thousand,
   eight hundred twenty-six

5. forty-seven thousand,
   four hundred eight

6. three hundred thirty-five thousand,
   two hundred forty-seven

7. two hundred fourteen thousand,
   six hundred nineteen

8. sixty-six thousand,
   one hundred fifty-two

9. twenty-eight thousand,
   nine hundred eighty-three

10. six hundred forty-two thousand,
   seven hundred six

A. 214,619

B. 94,304

C. 75,826

D. 335,247

E. 83,976

F. 66,152

G. 642,706

H. 462,510

I. 47,408

J. 28,983

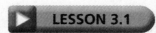

Missing Numbers

Detective Casey needs to find some missing numbers. Can you help her? When you find them, circle the numbers so she knows where to look. The numbers can be found going up, across, down, backward, and diagonally.

1	2	8	6	7	4	3	0	5
5	0	1	9	4	2	1	8	9
2	2	7	8	0	1	3	6	4
4	8	7	5	2	6	0	4	3
7	5	1	4	6	2	1	0	8
4	6	9	8	2	0	3	4	7
9	8	5	2	4	3	0	1	6
2	9	3	7	4	6	5	0	9
1	7	2	8	3	9	6	4	5

1. 17,283	**2.** 50,194	**3.** 3,756
4. 27,423	**5.** 44,104	**6.** 4,301
7. 9,820	**8.** 5,469	**9.** 94,387
10. 9,132	**11.** 6,150	**12.** 7,402
13. 31,301	**14.** 28,674	**15.** 5,820

Detective Casey thanks you for all your hard work in helping her find the missing numbers.

Name _____

Model Numbers

Look at the models below. Under each, write the number that the model represents. When you finish, follow the directions at the bottom of the page.

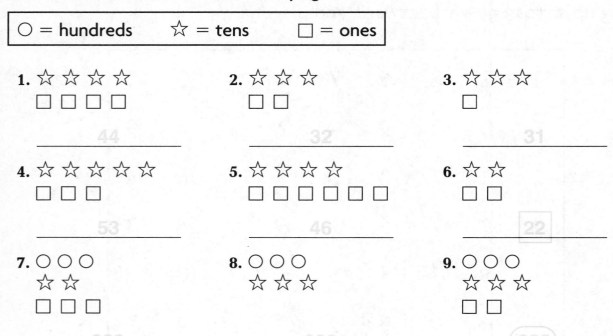

○ = hundreds ☆ = tens □ = ones

1. ☆ ☆ ☆ ☆
□ □ □ □
_____44_____

2. ☆ ☆ ☆
□ □
_____32_____

3. ☆ ☆ ☆
□
_____31_____

4. ☆ ☆ ☆ ☆ ☆
□ □ □
_____53_____

5. ☆ ☆ ☆ ☆
□ □ □ □ □ □
_____46_____

6. ☆ ☆
□ □
| 22 |

7. ○ ○ ○
☆ ☆
□ □ □
_____323_____

8. ○ ○ ○
☆ ☆ ☆
_____330_____

9. ○ ○ ○
☆ ☆ ☆
□ □
（332）

10. In Exercises 1–9, circle the answer that is the greatest number.

11. In Exercises 1–9, what is the number that is closest in size to the greatest number?
_____330_____

12. In Exercises 1–9, put a square around the answer that is the least number.

13. In Exercises 1–9, what is the number that is closest in size to the least number?
_____31_____

14. Choose your own number. Write what that number is, and model it by using circles, stars, and squares.

Check students' answers.

Scrambled Numbers!

Pick numbers from each circle to make three different
4-digit numbers. Write your numbers on the lines to the
left of the circle. Then, on the lines to the right of the
circle, put your numbers in order from least to greatest.
Students' answers will vary for all problems.

1. _____

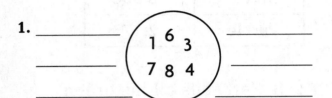

2. _____

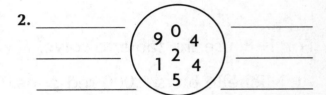

3. _____

4. _____

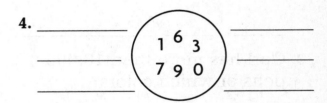

5. _____

6. _____

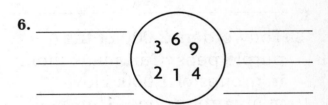

7. _____

8. _____

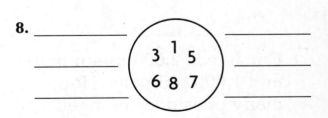

9. What is the greatest number
you came up with?

_____ Answers will vary.

10. What is the least number you
came up with?

_____ Answers will vary.

Table Talk

Carl's Pen Store expects a busy year. The table shows how many pens Carl has in his store.

Carl's Pen Store	
Blue	29,492
Red	13,650
Green	9,834
Black	6,500
Purple	2,173

For 1–8, use the table to solve.

1. Michelle buys 1,000 red pens. How many red pens does Carl have left?

   12,650 pens

2. If Carl sells all his green, black, and purple pens, how many pens will he sell in all?

   18,507 pens

3. Carl has more than 10,000 pens of which colors?

   blue and red

4. John needs 2,000 purple pens. Are there enough at Carl's Pen Store?

   yes

5. Tony orders 2,000 of the purple pens. Carl mails them in groups of 1,000. How many groups does Carl mail to Tony?

   2 groups

6. Amy needs to buy 7,000 black pens. She goes to Carl's store and buys all his black pens. How many pens does she still need to buy?

   500 pens

7. Eric needs 2,000 green pens and 1,000 red pens. How many pens does he need in all?

   3,000 pens

8. Carl mails all his blue pens to California. He can only fit 10,000 pens in a box. How many boxes will he need?

   3 boxes

Quick Sale

George's General Merchandise is having a sale. Each sale table will hold items that have been rounded to the nearest ten or hundred dollars for a quick sale. Under each item, write the table it should go on.

Table A $20 Table B $30 Table C $40 Table D $50

Table E $100 Table F $200 Table G $300 Table H $400

1.  $189

Table F

2. $25

Table B

3.  $175

Table F

4. $23

Table A

5.  $187

Table F

6.  $259

Table G

7.  $37

Table C

8.  $157

Table F

9.  $313

Table G

10. $45

Table D

11. $44

Table C

12. $113

Table E

Name _____

Round and Round We Go!

Look at the table at the bottom of the page. Round the three-digit numbers to the nearest hundred and the four-digit numbers to the nearest thousand. Then find the heart that has the rounded number. Use the code in the table to color it.

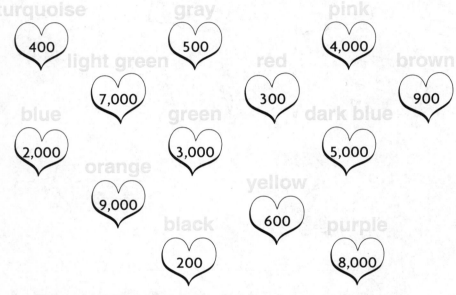

Number	Rounded Number	Color
256	300	red
1,678	2,000	blue
3,345	3,000	green
632	600	yellow
7,519	8,000	purple
8,881	9,000	orange
853	900	brown
3,780	4,000	pink
472	500	gray
187	200	black
4,574	5,000	dark blue
6,961	7,000	light green
390	400	turquoise

Name _____

Nature's Numbers

1. Mr. Jackson bought a globe and a bird feeder. About how much money did he spend?

   _____about $90_____

2. Mrs. Wilson bought a whale shirt, a stuffed penguin, and a bear book. About how much money did she spend?

   _____about $60_____

3. Ms. Garcia spent about $50. She bought a bear book and a

   _____stuffed penguin_____.

4. Mr. Curtis spent about $80. He bought a microscope and a

   _____whale shirt_____.

5. Ms. Hunter spent about $100. She bought a whale shirt, binoculars, and a

   _____stuffed penguin_____.

6. Mr. Vasquez spent about $70. He bought binoculars and a

   _____whale shirt_____.

7. You can spend about $80 at the gift shop. You want to buy 3 gifts that are all different. You could buy:

Possible answers are given.

_____shirt_____, _____book_____, and _____globe_____ or

_____shirt_____, _____bird feeder_____, and _____penguin_____.

Addition with Regrouping

Fill in the empty squares by adding the numbers across
each row, and adding the numbers down each column.

1.

+		
267	389	656
119	437	556
386	826	1,212

2.

+		
385	263	648
263	619	882
648	882	1,530

3.

+		
378	225	603
417	318	735
795	543	1,338

4.

+		
473	484	957
387	139	526
860	623	1,483

5.

+		
317	444	761
555	379	934
872	823	1,695

6.

+		
569	385	954
199	499	698
768	884	1,652

7.

+		
185	365	550
276	392	668
461	757	1,218

8.

+		
737	199	936
169	677	846
906	876	1,782

Palindromes

A *palindrome* is a word or phrase that reads the same forward and backward. Some examples are *Otto*, *Ada*, and *Madam, I'm Adam*.

Numbers can also be palindromes. Some examples are 88, 151, and 34,143. You can make your own number palindromes using addition. Look at the boxes.

Choose any 2- or 3-digit number. Reverse the digits.
$\begin{array}{r} 14 \\ +41 \\ \hline \end{array}$
Add. $\quad 55$
55 is a palindrome. It reads the same forward and backward.

Choose any 2- or 3-digit number. Reverse the digits. $\quad \begin{array}{r} 48 \\ +84 \\ \hline \end{array}$
Add. $\quad 132$
Reverse the digits of the sum. Add. $\quad \begin{array}{r} 132 \\ +231 \\ \hline 363 \end{array}$
The number 363 is a palindrome.

Reverse and add until you get a palindrome.

1. $\begin{array}{r} 57 \\ +75 \\ \hline 132 \\ +231 \\ \hline 363 \end{array}$	2. $\begin{array}{r} 153 \\ +351 \\ \hline 504 \\ +405 \\ \hline 909 \end{array}$	3. $\begin{array}{r} 29 \\ +92 \\ \hline 121 \end{array}$	4. $\begin{array}{r} 261 \\ +162 \\ \hline 423 \\ +324 \\ \hline 747 \end{array}$

Try this out with your own 2- or 3-digit numbers. For some numbers, you need to reverse and add many times before you get a palindrome. You may need an extra piece of paper. Check students' work. Answers will vary.

5.	6.	7.	8. A 3-digit combination of 7, 8, & 9 will not work.

Name_____

Get in Shape

For each pair of number sentences, each shape represents a single number. You may use the strategy *predict and test* to figure out the number that each shape represents. Write the number inside the shape.

Example:

$(7) + [5] = 12$

$(7) - [5] = 2$

1.

$(9) + \triangle 6 = 15$

$(9) - \triangle 6 = 3$

2.

$(15) + [5] = 20$

$(15) - [5] = 10$

3.

$(80) + [20] = 100$

$(80) - [20] = 60$

4.

$(9) + \triangle 4 = 13$

$(9) - \triangle 4 = 5$

5.

$\triangle 4 + [3] = 7$

$\triangle 4 - 1 = [3]$

6.

$(9) + \triangle 7 = 16$

$(9) - 2 = \triangle 7$

Answers will vary.

For Problems 7–8, there is more than one possible solution.

7.

$\triangle + [\ ] = 10$

$10 - [\ ] = \triangle$

8.

$8 - \triangle = (\ )$

$8 - (\ ) = \triangle$

Name _____

Add Greater Numbers

Fill in the missing digits. Possible answers are given for Exercises 4, 10, and 20.

1.
```
  3, 4 7 7
+ 4, 1 7 6
―――――――
  7, 6 5 3
```

2.
```
  2, 9 3 5
+ 3, 7 8 2
―――――――
  6, 7 1 7
```

3.
```
  1, 6 3 8
+ 6, 2 8 4
―――――――
  7, 9 2 2
```

4.
```
  4, 0 2 1
+ 4, 1 9 3
―――――――
  8, 2 1 4
```

5.
```
  8, 5 1 6
+ 1, 3 9 8
―――――――
  9, 9 1 4
```

6.
```
  2, 8 2 8
+ 5, 3 5 3
―――――――
  8, 1 8 1
```

7.
```
   6, 4 0 2
 + 4, 9 7 6
―――――――
  11, 3 7 8
```

8.
```
  4, 5 8 8
+ 3, 2 1 9
―――――――
  7, 8 0 7
```

9.
```
  5, 1 8 9
+ 2, 3 0 3
―――――――
  7, 4 9 2
```

10.
```
  3, 7 3 7
+ 4, 6 4 6
―――――――
  8, 3 8 3
```

11.
```
  2, 7 9 1
+ 4, 1 7 1
―――――――
  6, 9 6 2
```

12.
```
  5, 7 2 9
+ 4, 1 7 3
―――――――
  9, 9 0 2
```

13.
```
  3, 2 3 5
+ 6, 3 7 1
―――――――
  9, 6 0 6
```

14.
```
  1, 3 5 7
+ 2, 4 6 8
―――――――
  3, 8 2 5
```

15.
```
   8, 8 8 5
 + 4, 4 4 4
―――――――
  1 3, 3 2 9
```

16.
```
  5, 2 5 8
+ 2, 8 4 8
―――――――
  8, 1 0 6
```

17.
```
  7, 8 0 2
+ 1, 5 5 6
―――――――
  9, 3 5 8
```

18.
```
  3, 8 2 4
+ 2, 1 7 6
―――――――
  6, 0 0 0
```

19.
```
  2, 0 9 3
+ 5, 3 7 6
―――――――
  7, 4 6 9
```

20.
```
  4, 1 7 5
+ 3, 4 7 8
―――――――
  7, 6 5 3
```

21.
```
  5, 4 7 9
+ 4, 1 8 1
―――――――
  9, 6 6 0
```

Challenge CW23

Write Expressions and Number Sentences

Write the missing number that completes the sentence.
Find the code letter for each answer in the code box
below. Write the code letter under each answer. Your
answers will solve a riddle.

$18 + \boxed{} = 44$ $15 = \boxed{} - 12$ $\boxed{} + 48 = 62$ $120 = 20 + \boxed{}$

26   27   14   100
P   L   E   A

$\boxed{} - 45 = 45$ $56 - \boxed{} = 42$ $33 + 44 = \boxed{}$ $162 - 135 = \boxed{}$

90   14   77   27
S   E   L

$\boxed{} - 9 = 5$ $16 + 123 = \boxed{}$ $\boxed{} - 32 = 107$ $\boxed{} - 123 = 15$

14   139   139   138
E   T   T   U

$\boxed{} - 15 = 4$ $\boxed{} + 53 = 67$ $\boxed{} - 14 = 63$ $123 - \boxed{} = 23$

19   14   77   100
C   E   A

$\boxed{} - 17 = 10$ $\boxed{} + 77 = 99$ $353 = \boxed{} - 16$ $\boxed{} + 124 = 138$

27   22   369   14
L   O   N   E

100 = A	337 = B	19 = C	77 = (space)
14 = E	22 = O	138 = U	283 = H
75 = J	139 = T	27 = L	108 = M
369 = N	26 = P	80 = R	90 = S

What did the rabbits say when the farmer caught them
in his garden?

Please lettuce alone.

Estimate Differences

Work with a partner.

Materials:
- one number cube, with numbers 0–5
- one number cube, with numbers 1–6
- one number cube, with numbers 4–9

How to Play:
The object of the game is to get the greatest number of points.

Step 1 The first player rolls the three number cubes. This person arranges the cubes to make a 3-digit number. This person also rounds the number to the nearest hundred and writes it down.

Step 2 The second player rolls the three number cubes. This person arranges the cubes to make a 3-digit number that can be subtracted from the number the first player wrote down.

Step 3 The first player rounds that 3-digit number to the nearest hundred and subtracts it from the number that was written down.

Step 4 The answer to the estimated difference is the number of points the first player gets.

Take turns repeating Steps 1–4.

After playing the game, answer these questions.

1. What strategies did you use?

   Possible answer: When I was the first player, I tried to make my 3-digit number the greatest number possible. When I was the second player, I tried to make the number subtracted the greatest number possible.

2. What was the most difficult part of playing this game?

   Possible answer: It was hard to decide which 3-digit number to make for my partner to subtract. I had to be sure my partner would get the least number of points possible.

Subtraction Puzzles

Fill in the empty squares by subtracting the numbers across each row and subtracting the numbers down each column.

1. ⊖

467	289	178
119	68	51
348	221	127

2. ⊖

585	299	286
263	159	104
322	140	182

3. ⊖

476	288	188
318	169	149
158	119	39

4. ⊖

463	184	279
287	39	248
176	145	31

5. ⊖

617	344	273
355	179	176
262	165	97

6. ⊖

569	285	284
311	196	115
258	89	169

7. ⊖

485	167	318
272	163	109
213	4	209

8. ⊖

733	377	356
466	179	287
267	198	69

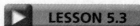

Riddle Ride

Find each difference. Then look at the rows of boxes at the bottom of the page. Find the two numbers that the difference falls between. In the box between those two numbers, write the letter that is next to the difference.

Example:

$$\begin{array}{r} 566 \\ -199 \\ \hline 367 \end{array} \quad \textbf{G}$$

$\begin{array}{r} 956 \\ -280 \\ \hline 676 \end{array}$ **T**	$\begin{array}{r} 424 \\ -218 \\ \hline 206 \end{array}$ **Y**	$\begin{array}{r} 613 \\ -272 \\ \hline 341 \end{array}$ **N**	$\begin{array}{r} 430 \\ -385 \\ \hline 45 \end{array}$ **A**
$\begin{array}{r} 613 \\ -438 \\ \hline 175 \end{array}$ **L**	$\begin{array}{r} 756 \\ -255 \\ \hline 501 \end{array}$ **R**	$\begin{array}{r} 900 \\ -261 \\ \hline 639 \end{array}$ **E**	$\begin{array}{r} 425 \\ -126 \\ \hline 299 \end{array}$ **I**
$\begin{array}{r} 525 \\ -\ 68 \\ \hline 457 \end{array}$ **A**	$\begin{array}{r} 802 \\ -242 \\ \hline 560 \end{array}$ **P**	$\begin{array}{r} 720 \\ -285 \\ \hline 435 \end{array}$ **C**	$\begin{array}{r} 456 \\ -344 \\ \hline 112 \end{array}$ **F**

What kind of pet can you take a ride on?

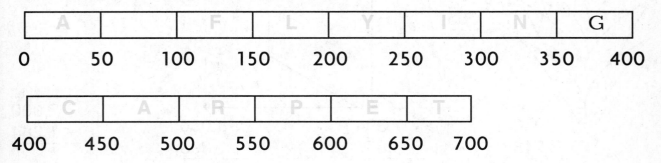

Subtract 3- and 4-Digit Numbers

Subtract. Connect the dots in order from the least difference to the greatest difference.

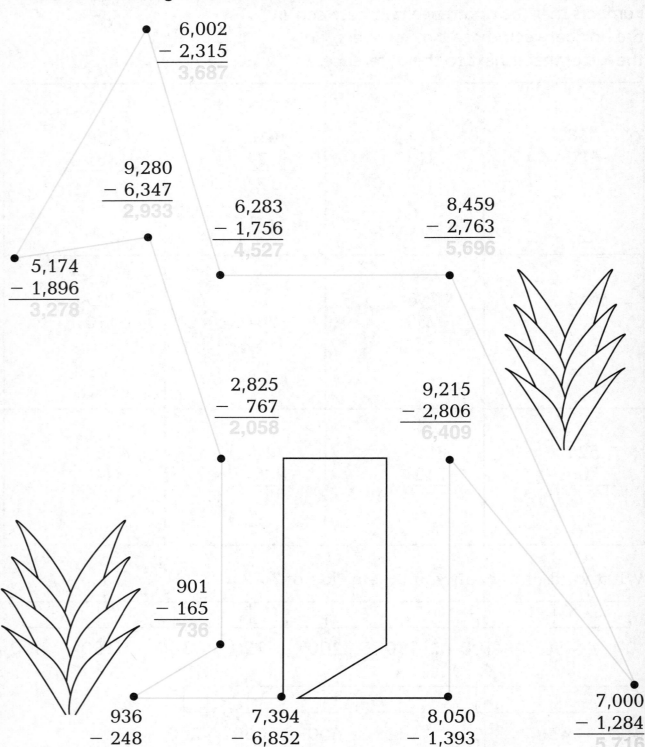

6,002
− 2,315
3,687

9,280
− 6,347
2,933

6,283
− 1,756
4,527

8,459
− 2,763
5,696

5,174
− 1,896
3,278

2,825
−   767
2,058

9,215
− 2,806
6,409

901
− 165
736

936
− 248
688

7,394
− 6,852
542

8,050
− 1,393
6,657

7,000
− 1,284
5,716

Missing Digits

Fill in the missing digits.

1.
```
  1, 3 0 0
-    1 2 5
  ─────────
  1, 1 7 5
```

2.
```
  1, 5 0 0
-    3 2 7
  ─────────
  1, 1 7 3
```

3.
```
  3, 9 0 0
- 3, 6 3 4
  ─────────
     2 6 6
```

4.
```
  5, 5 0 3
-    1 9 8
  ─────────
  5, 3 0 5
```

5.
```
  2, 6 0 1
-    2 8 4
  ─────────
  2, 3 1 7
```

6.
```
  6, 7 0 7
- 1, 1 4 9
  ─────────
  5, 5 5 8
```

7.
```
  2, 4 0 0
- 2, 1 9 5
  ─────────
     2 0 5
```

8.
```
  7, 7 0 0
- 5, 3 3 2
  ─────────
  2, 3 6 8
```

9.
```
  1, 0 4 0
-    3 9 0
  ─────────
     6 5 0
```

Find the difference. Then check by adding.

```
  5, 0 0 6        1, 2 5 1
- 1, 2 5 1      + 3, 7 5 5
  ─────────       ─────────
  3, 7 5 5        5, 0 0 6
```

```
  7, 0 0 4        3, 5 9 3
- 3, 5 9 3      + 3, 4 1 1
  ─────────       ─────────
  3, 4 1 1        7, 0 0 4
```

```
  3, 4 0 7        3, 2 7 8
-    1 2 9      +    1 2 9
  ─────────       ─────────
  3, 2 7 8        3, 4 0 7
```

```
  9, 0 2 9        7, 6 7 7
- 1, 3 5 2      + 1, 3 5 2
  ─────────       ─────────
  7, 6 7 7        9, 0 2 9
```

Challenge   CW29

Planning a Party

Mrs. Laff is catering a party for 14 girls and 14 boys. Use the chart to help her plan the party.

Cupcakes	16 in a box
Pizza	1 pizza has 8 slices
Lemonade	1 bottle fills 10 glasses
Chips	9 servings in a bag
Balloons	12 in a bag

1. Each person will get 1 cupcake. How many boxes of cupcakes are needed?

   _____ 2 boxes _____

2. How many cupcakes will be left if each person eats one cupcake?

   _____ 4 _____

3. How many pizzas would give each person 2 slices?

   _____ 7 pizzas _____

4. How many bottles of lemonade would give each person 2 glasses of lemonade?

   _____ 6 bottles of lemonade

5. Mrs. Laff bought 3 bags of chips. About how many servings per person is this?

   _____ about 1 serving _____

6. Mrs. Laff plans to make a name card for each person. How many name cards must she make?

   _____ 28 _____

7. Mrs. Laff plans to decorate the party room with balloons. She wants to use at least 50 balloons. How many bags should she buy?

   _____ 5 bags _____

8. A package of party napkins costs $8.85. Mrs. Laff pays for the napkins with $10. How much change will she get?

   _____ $1.15 _____

9. Mrs. Laff has $120 to spend on food for this party. The cupcakes will cost $32.85. The pizza will cost $48.00. The lemonade will cost $8.19. The chips will cost $10.94. Will she need more money for the food? Explain.

   No; because $30 + $50 + $10 + $10 = $100, which is less than $120.

10. Mrs. Laff can arrange the tables in 3 different ways. Each way seats a different number of people. She is able to seat 20, 25, or 36. Which way should she arrange her tables? Explain.

    Since she needs seats for 28, she will have to arrange the tables to seat 36.

Colorful Sets

Use this key to color the design below.

Section A and all sections with equivalent sets of money	Red
Section B and all sections with equivalent sets of money	Yellow
Section C and all sections with equivalent sets of money	Green
Section D and all sections with equivalent sets of money	Blue

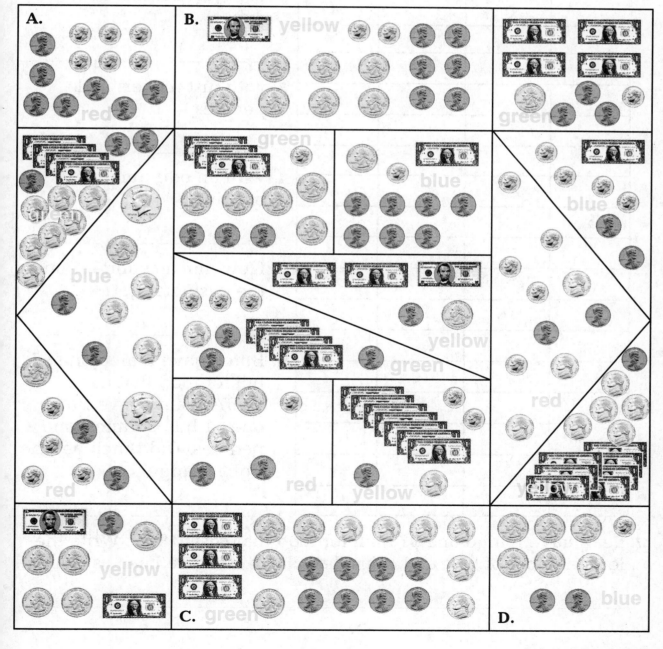

Name _____

LESSON 6.2

Making Change

Elaine works at a fast-food restaurant. A customer gives her one $5 bill to pay for food that costs $4.66. How many different ways can she make change?

Complete the table.

1.

Quarters	Dimes	Nickels	Pennies
1	0	0	9
1	0	1	4
0	3	0	4
0	2	2	4
0	2	1	9
0	2	0	14
0	1	4	4
0	1	3	9
0	1	2	14
0	1	1	19
0	1	0	24
0	0	1	29
0	0	2	24
0	0	3	19
0	0	4	14
0	0	5	9
0	0	6	4
0	0	0	34

Write how many different ways she can make change.

2. with just nickels and dimes

_____ 0 _____

3. with just nickels and pennies

_____ 6 _____

4. with an odd number of coins

_____ 6 _____

5. How much change should the customer get?

_____ 34¢ _____

6. Butch gave Elaine one $5 bill for food that costs $3.67. Elaine gave Butch one $1 bill, 3 dimes, and 3 pennies. Did Butch get the right change?

_____ yes _____

7. Leah gave Elaine one $10 bill for food that costs $8.29. Write the least number of bills and coins that Elaine can give Leah as change.

one $1 bill, 2 quarters, 2 dimes, and 1 penny or one $1 bill, 1 half-dollar, 2 dimes, and 1 penny

CW32 Challenge

Shopping at the Pet Store

 $1.49 $0.46    $0.89    $0.33    $2.98

1. Jim has

Does Jim have enough
money to buy a brush?

_____ no _____

2. Carrie has

Does Carrie have enough
money to buy 2 cans of cat
food?

_____ yes _____

3. Lisa has

How much more money does
Lisa need to buy a bowl?

_____ $0.14 _____

4. Fred has

How much money will Fred
have left if he buys a can of
cat food?

_____ $0.25 _____

5. Jane pays for a toy mouse
with 8 coins. What coins does
she use?

___ 3 quarters, 1 dime, 4 pennies ___

_____

6. Paul pays for a ball with
4 coins. What coins does
he use?

___ 1 quarter, 2 dimes, 1 penny ___

_____

Name _____

Make Change

Complete the table of items needed to make a cake.

Paid	Cost of Item	Change Received
(8 quarters)	$0.74	$0.06
(2 one-dollar bills)	$1.29	$0.71
Possible answer: $5.00	$1.49	$3.51
Possible answer: $1.00	$0.65	$0.35
(1 one-dollar bill, 1 quarter)	$1.05	$0.20
(4 quarters, 1 nickel)	$1.09	$0.01
(2 one-dollar bills, 2 quarters)	$2.35	$0.15

CW34   Challenge

Money Madness

Write the missing numbers.

1. $ 2 . 5 5
    + 1 . 9 8
    ─────────
    $ [4] . 5 [3]

2. $ 2 . 9 5
    + 3 . [6] 9
    ─────────
    $ 6 . 6 4

3. $ 4 . 5 9
    + [2] . 3 [9]
    ─────────
    $ 6 . 9 8

4. $ 2 3 . [9] 1
    + [1] 5 . 3 9
    ─────────
    $ 3 9 . 3 0

5. $ 3 . 9 5
    − 1 . 4 9
    ─────────
    $ [2] . 4 [6]

6. $ 4 . 5 0
    − 1 . [2] 8
    ─────────
    $ 3 . 2 2

7. $ 6 . 5 9
    − [1] . 9 [2]
    ─────────
    $ 4 . 6 7

8. $ 4 0 . [7] 5
    − 2 [1] . 4 9
    ─────────
    $ 1 9 . 2 6

For problems 9–12, use the table.

Sandwiches	
Ham	$3.89
Cheese	$2.35
Chicken	$3.19
Peanut butter and jelly	$1.65

9. Bob buys 2 peanut butter and jelly sandwiches. Should he give the clerk a $1 bill, a $5 bill, or a $10 bill? Explain.

   Possible answer: a $5 bill
   because the cost is between
   $3.00 and $4.00

10. Joan buys a sandwich. She gives the clerk a $5 bill. Her change is $2.65. What kind of sandwich does she buy?

    cheese

11. Mr. Riley buys one of each kind of sandwich. How much should he give the clerk?

    $11.08

12. Make up your own problem about sandwiches you will buy for yourself and a friend. Write the problem so that the solver must use estimation, addition, and subtraction. Have a classmate solve it.

    Check students' problems. Sample answer: I have $6.00 to
    buy 2 sandwiches, one for me and one for my friend Ben.
    Which sandwiches can I buy? How much change will I get?

Find the Time

Read the time on each clock. For each time, draw a line to connect the words and numbers that you used. The words and numbers may go up, down, left, right, or diagonal. The first one is done for you.

1.    **2.**    **3.**    **4.**

5.    **6.**    **7.**    **8.**

25 minutes	eight	before	17 minutes	quarter
after	after	ten	past	past
two	eight	three	before	seven
before	35 minutes	quarter	nine	13 minutes
half	to	two	five	8 minutes
one	past	before	after	before
half	52 minutes	seven	6 minutes	eleven

Time for a Riddle

To solve the riddle, match the letter in the circle and the time in the box below. Write the letter on the line above the box.

1. At 15 minutes after nine, I start school. (l)

2. At four thirty I had soccer practice. (a)

3. I get out of school when it is 30 minutes after three. (f)

4. I have music class at 30 minutes after two. (b)

5. I eat dinner at 15 minutes before six. (s)

6. At six fifteen my alarm wakes me up. (a)

7. We looked up at the moon at eight forty-five. (u)

8. I have a doctor's appointment at 30 minutes after ten. (o)

9. By twelve forty-five we had the lunch dishes put away. (n)

10. When it is ten thirty, my mom is asleep. (n)

11. I had to get ready for bed at 30 minutes after eight. (c)

12. We looked for a star at ten forty-five. (s)

13. When it was 15 minutes before four, I played baseball with my friends. (e)

14. When it was 15 minutes after one, I awoke to the sound of thunder. (d)

15. At three fifteen I will visit my friend. (t)

16. I have never stayed awake later than eleven thirty. (e)

17. The sun will rise tomorrow at five fifteen. (g)

18. When I was sick, I slept until 15 minutes after eleven. (h)

What has a __f__ __a__ __c__ __e__ and __h__ __a__ __n__ __d__ __s__

| 3:30 P.M. | 6:15 A.M. | 8:30 P.M. | 3:45 P.M. | | 11:15 A.M. | 4:30 P.M. | 10:30 P.M. | 1:15 A.M. | 5:45 P.M. |

__b__ __u__ __t__ __n__ __o__ __l__ __e__ __g__ __s__ ?

| 2:30 P.M. | 8:45 P.M. | 3:15 P.M. | | 12:45 P.M. | 10:30 A.M. | | 9:15 A.M. | 11:30 P.M. | 5:15 A.M. | 10:45 P.M. |

Solve the riddle. _____a clock_____

Name _____

Time Flies

What do pilot rabbits fly?

Use the clocks to answer the riddle. Find the clock that matches each time written at the bottom of the page. Write the letter of the clock in the box above the time.

A	L	S	E
N	H	P	R

H	A	R	E
15 minutes after 9:15	1 hour after 7:30	30 minutes after 4:15	1 hour 15 minutes after 10:00

P	L	A	N	E	S
15 minutes after 9:45	30 minutes after 11:45	15 minutes after 8:15	45 minutes after 1:30	30 minutes after 10:45	45 minutes after 3:15

Name _____

Make a Schedule

Mr. Frank's class is going to a nature center. Mr. Frank
drew these clocks to show when each activity begins.
Each activity ends just as the next activity begins.

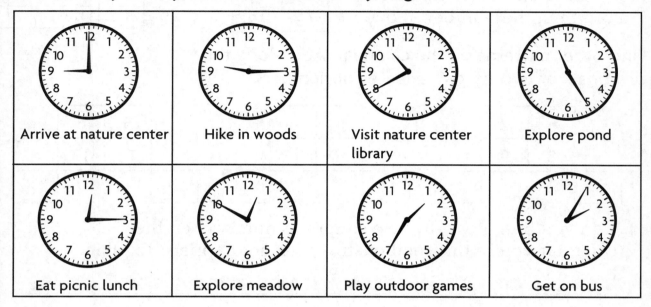

Arrive at nature center	Hike in woods	Visit nature center library	Explore pond
Eat picnic lunch	Explore meadow	Play outdoor games	Get on bus

1. Complete this schedule.

Activity	Time	Elapsed Time
Arrive	9:00 A.M.–9:15 A.M.	15 minutes
Hike	9:15 A.M.–10:40 A.M.	1 hour 25 minutes
Visit library	10:40 A.M.–11:25 A.M.	45 minutes
Explore pond	11:25 A.M.–12:15 P.M.	50 minutes
Eat lunch	12:15 P.M.–12:50 P.M.	35 minutes
Explore meadow	12:50 P.M.–1:35 P.M.	45 minutes
Play games	1:35 P.M.–2:05 P.M.	30 minutes

2. Which activity lasts the longest? _____ hike _____

3. How much time in all will the class spend at the

nature center? _____ 5 hours 5 minutes _____

Calendar Challenge

Sam cut out a column of numbers from his calendar.

He noticed that each number is 7 more than the number above it.

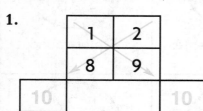

4

11   4 + 7 = 11

18   11 + 7 = 18

25   18 + 7 = 25

MARCH

S	M	T	W	T	F	S
	1	2	3	4	5	6
7	8	9	10	11	12	13
14	15	16	17	18	19	20
21	22	23	24	25	26	27
28	29	30	31			

Find other patterns on the calendar. Add along the diagonals of two-by-two squares of numbers.

1.

1	2
8	9

10   10

2.

3	4
10	11

14   14

3.

5	6
12	13

18   18

4. Can you find a two-by-two square of numbers on the calendar where this relationship does not happen? Explain.

No; the sums of the diagonals of each of the possible

two-by-two squares of numbers are always the same.

Add along the diagonals of three-by-three squares of numbers.

5.

1	2	3
8	9	10
15	16	17

27   27

6.

4	5	6
11	12	13
18	19	20

36   36

7.

7	8	9
14	15	16
21	22	23

45   45

8. Can you find a three-by-three square of numbers on the calendar where this relationship does not happen? Explain.

No; the sums of the diagonals of each of the possible three-by-

three squares of numbers are always the same.

9. Add the diagonals of a four-by-four square of numbers on the calendar. What do you notice?

The sums are the same.

State Facts

The table shows when some places in the United States became states. Add points to the time line for each state in the table. The finished time line will show the order in which the places became states.

STATEHOOD			
State	**Year**	**State**	**Year**
Colorado	1876	Minnesota	1858
Florida	1845	Missouri	1821
Illinois	1818	Nevada	1864
Michigan	1837	North Dakota	1889

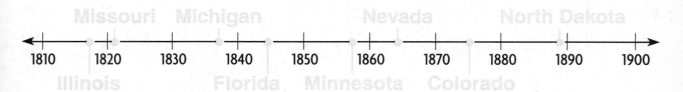

Missouri   Michigan   Nevada   North Dakota

←—|——|——————|——|——|——————|——|——————|——————|——|——————|——→
1810   1820   1830   1840   1850   1860   1870   1880   1890   1900

Illinois   Florida   Minnesota   Colorado

Write the states in time order in the boxes below. Write the first state to become a state in box one, the second state in box two, and so on. The first one is done for you.

1. **Illinois** _____ has the tallest building in the United States.

2. Missouri _____ is the state where the first ice-cream cone is believed to have been sold.

3. Michigan _____ borders on the largest lake in the United States.

4. Florida _____ has orange juice as its official state beverage.

5. Minnesota _____ has more than 15,000 lakes.

6. Nevada _____ usually gets less rain than any other state.

7. Colorado _____ has more mountains higher than 14,000 feet than any other state.

8. North Dakota _____ is an important wheat-growing state.

Name _____

Multiply in the Sky

Isabel is on her first airplane flight. She looks out the window and writes down what she sees. Complete each number sentence. Then draw a picture of what Isabel sees. Possible answers are given. Check students' drawings.

1. $3 \times 3 =$ ___9 houses___   2. $2 \times 2 =$ ___4 trucks___

3. $4 \times 5 =$ ___20 trees___   4. $2 \times 4 =$ ___8 cars___

5. $3 \times 2 =$ ___6 swing sets___

Pattern Plot

Find the next numbers.
Write a rule used to make the pattern. Possible rules are given.

1. 22, 24, 26, 28, ___30___, ___32___, ___34___, ___36___

Rule: _____add 2_____

2. 80, 85, 90, 95, ___100___, ___105___, ___110___, ___115___

Rule: _____add 5_____

3. 117, 122, 127, 132, ___137___, ___142___, ___147___, ___152___

Rule: _____add 5_____

4. 211, 213, 215, 217, ___219___, ___221___, ___223___, ___225___

Rule: _____add 2_____

5. 317, 319, 324, 326, 331, 333, 338, 340,
345, ___347___, ___352___, ___354___, ___359___, ___361___

Rule: _____add 2, then add 5_____

Make up your own pattern using differences of 2 or 5.
Write your rule under your pattern. Patterns will vary.
Check students' work.

6. _____, _____, _____, _____, _____, _____, _____

Rule: _____

7. _____, _____, _____, _____, _____, _____, _____

Rule: _____

Dance on Arrays

You have been asked to complete a design for a dance floor using arrays of colors. You can use as much red, green, blue, yellow, and orange as you want. Make a list of the colors and arrays you use. The design has been started for you in black. Designs will vary. Check to see that students have made accurate multiplication equations for the arrays they colored.

$2 \times 2 =$ ___4___ black squares

_____ $\times$ _____ = _____

_____ $\times$ _____ = _____

_____ $\times$ _____ = _____

_____ $\times$ _____ = _____

_____ $\times$ _____ = _____

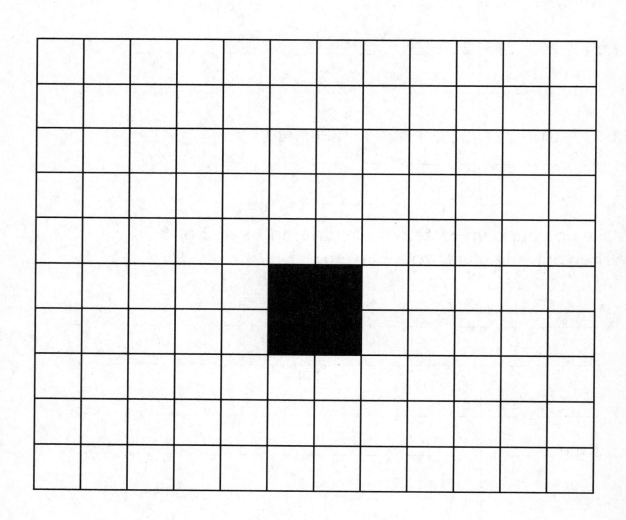

Puzzling Products

Find the product in Column 2 for each problem in Column 1.
Then write the letter of the product on the line in front of
the problem.

Column 1   **Column 2**

___N___ **1.** 9×3 (A) 18

___S___ **2.** 5×5 (B) 8

___B___ **3.** 2×4 (D) 24

___Y___ **4.** 7×3 (E) 15

___E___ **5.** 3×5 (M) 10

___U___ **6.** 8×2 (N) 27

___A___ **7.** 6×3 (O) 6

___M___ **8.** 2×5 (R) 30

___D___ **9.** 3×8 (S) 25

___R___ **10.** 5×6 (U) 16

___O___ **11.** 2×3 (Y) 21

Use your answers to decode the sentence below. The
problem number is under each line. Write the letter of
your answer from Column 1 on the line.

A D D E N D S   A R E
7 9 9 5 1 9 2   7 10 5

N U M B E R S   Y O U   A D D .
1 6 8 3 5 10 2   4 11 6   7 9 9

What's the Question?

For 1–6, complete the problem with a question so that the
answer given is correct. Possible questions are given.

1. Four friends walked 4 blocks
   to school. Each one is
   carrying 3 books.

   How many books are there?
   _____

   Too much information;

   12 books

2. Doug bought 6 pencils. They
   were on sale today for 5¢ less
   than they were yesterday.

   How much did he spend

   on pencils?

   Not enough information
   _____

3. Xavier bought 4 ice-cream
   cones. The clerk gave him
   $0.50 in change.

   How much did he spend

   on ice-cream cones?

   Not enough information
   _____

4. Misty's piggy bank has
   3 times as many nickels as
   dimes. She has 3 more dimes
   than quarters. Misty has
   8 dimes.

   How many nickels does

   she have?

   Too much information;

   24 nickels

5. When all of Pam's cousins
   come to visit, the number of
   children in her house will
   double. Pam has 2 cousins.

   How many children will

   be in her house?

   Right amount of information

   4 children

6. A three-digit number has a
   ones digit that is 4 times its
   tens digit. The tens digit is 2.
   The hundreds digit is 1 less
   than the tens digit.

   What is the ones digit?
   _____

   _____

   Too much information; 8

Name _____

Fit Feasting Facts

The Food Guide Pyramid
is a guide to healthy
eating. It shows how to
build a healthy diet by
eating different kinds
of foods.

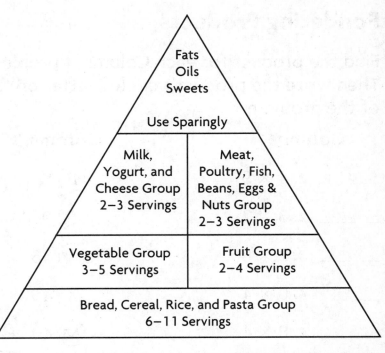

Use the Food Guide
Pyramid to answer
the questions below.

1. How many servings of fruit
   should you eat every day?

   2–4 servings

2. How many servings of bread,
   cereal, rice, and pasta should
   you eat every day?

   6–11 servings

3. Every day, Max eats the
   most servings of vegetables
   recommended by the Food
   Guide Pyramid. How many
   servings of vegetables does
   Max eat in a week?

   35 servings

4. Every day, Julie eats the
   fewest servings of bread,
   cereal, rice, and pasta
   recommended by the Food
   Guide Pyramid. How many
   servings from this group does
   Julie eat in 3 days?

   18 servings

5. Every day, Juan eats the least
   number of servings from the
   milk, yogurt, and cheese
   group shown in the pyramid.
   How many servings of this
   group does Juan eat in
   5 days?

   10 servings

6. Tamala eats the greatest
   number of servings of the
   meat, poultry, fish, beans,
   eggs, and nuts group every
   day. How many servings of
   this group does she eat in
   8 days?

   24 servings

Challenge CW47

Pondering Products

Find the product for each Column 1 problem in Column 2. Then write the product's circled letter on the line in front of the problem.

Column 1	Column 2
__I__ 1. 4×9	Ⓔ 8
__T__ 2. 3×2	Ⓕ 0
__O__ 3. 2×8	Ⓘ 36
__F__ 4. 0×4	Ⓧ 45
__R__ 5. 8×4	Ⓜ 40
__U__ 6. 5×7	Ⓝ 20
__E__ 7. 4×2	Ⓞ 16
__S__ 8. 2×7	Ⓡ 32
__X__ 9. 5×9	Ⓢ 14
__M__ 10. 8×5	Ⓣ 6
__N__ 11. 5×4	Ⓤ 35

Use your answers to decode the sentence below. The problem number under each blank tells you where to look in Column 1. Write the letter of your answer from Column 1 on the blank.

F O U R   T I M E S   F O U R
4. 3. 6. 5.   2. 1. 10. 7. 8.   4. 3. 6. 5.

I S   S I X T E E N .
1. 8.   8. 1. 9. 2. 7. 7. 11.

Problem Solving Strategy

Find a Pattern

Play with a partner.

Materials: three number cubes: one numbered 1–6, one numbered 7–12, and one numbered 13–18

How to Play:

Players take turns as rollers and pattern makers. The roller rolls the three number cubes and writes the three numbers in order from least to greatest on a line below under his or her partner's column of patterns.

The pattern maker finds a rule and continues the pattern for four more numbers. For example, for the numbers 5, 10, and 18, the rule could be (+ 5, + 8) or (× 2, + 8).

The seventh number in the pattern is the number of points the pattern maker scores. Find the sum of each player's seventh numbers. The winner is the player with the greater sum.

Player 1 Patterns	Player 2 Patterns
——, ——, ——, ——, ——, ——, ——	——, ——, ——, ——, ——, ——, ——
——, ——, ——, ——, ——, ——, ——	——, ——, ——, ——, ——, ——, ——
——, ——, ——, ——, ——, ——, ——	——, ——, ——, ——, ——, ——, ——
——, ——, ——, ——, ——, ——, ——	——, ——, ——, ——, ——, ——, ——
——, ——, ——, ——, ——, ——, ——	——, ——, ——, ——, ——, ——, ——
——, ——, ——, ——, ——, ——, ——	——, ——, ——, ——, ——, ——, ——

Player 1: Find the sum of the last numbers in each of your patterns.

Player 2: Find the sum of the last numbers in each of your patterns.

_____   _____

The Factor Game

Play with a partner.

Materials: 2 game tokens
30 number cards including ten 7s, ten 8s,
and ten 9s

How to Play:

Place the game tokens on Start. Shuffle the number cards. Turn the number cards upside down or place them in a bag.

Take turns drawing a number card. Move to the closest space with a missing factor that matches the number on the card. Write the factor in the space. The first player to reach Finish wins!

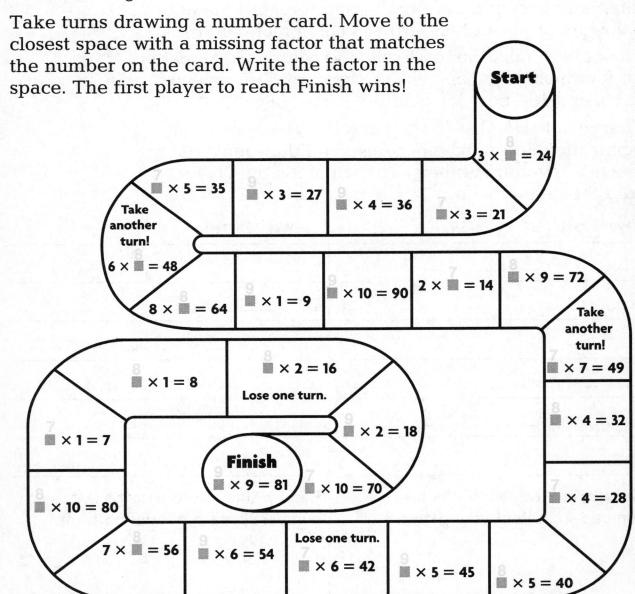

Start

$3 \times \blacksquare = 24$

$\blacksquare \times 5 = 35$

Take another turn!

$\blacksquare \times 3 = 27$

$\blacksquare \times 4 = 36$

$\blacksquare \times 3 = 21$

$6 \times \blacksquare = 48$

$8 \times \blacksquare = 64$

$\blacksquare \times 1 = 9$

$\blacksquare \times 10 = 90$

$2 \times \blacksquare = 14$

$\blacksquare \times 9 = 72$

Take another turn!

$\blacksquare \times 7 = 49$

$\blacksquare \times 4 = 32$

$\blacksquare \times 1 = 8$

$\blacksquare \times 2 = 16$

Lose one turn.

$\blacksquare \times 2 = 18$

$\blacksquare \times 1 = 7$

Finish

$\blacksquare \times 9 = 81$

$\blacksquare \times 10 = 70$

$\blacksquare \times 4 = 28$

$\blacksquare \times 10 = 80$

$7 \times \blacksquare = 56$

$\blacksquare \times 6 = 54$

Lose one turn.

$\blacksquare \times 6 = 42$

$\blacksquare \times 5 = 45$

$\blacksquare \times 5 = 40$

Algebra: Missing Factors

Find the missing number for each Section 1 problem in Section 2. Then write the number's circled letter on the line in front of the problem.

Section 1

__M__ 1. $2 \times \blacksquare = 8$ __I__ 9. $1 \times \blacksquare = 1$

__E__ 2. $\blacksquare \times 1 = 9$ __T__ 10. $7 \times \blacksquare = 21$

__A__ 3. $\blacksquare \times 5 = 40$ __S__ 11. $4 \times 7 = \blacksquare$

__B__ 4. $8 \times \blacksquare = 0$ __Z__ 12. $2 \times 8 = \blacksquare$

__N__ 5. $\blacksquare \times 4 = 24$ __O__ 13. $5 \times 7 = \blacksquare$

__U__ 6. $2 \times 6 = \blacksquare$ __Q__ 14. $4 \times 8 = \blacksquare$

__Y__ 7. $\blacksquare \times 4 = 20$ __L__ 15. $9 \times \blacksquare = 18$

__R__ 8. $\blacksquare \times 5 = 35$

Section 2

(N) 6   (E) 9

(A) 8   (I) 1

(L) 2   (Q) 32

(B) 0   (O) 35

(Y) 5   (M) 4

(T) 3   (Z) 16

(S) 28   (R) 7

(U) 12

Use your answers to decode the sentence below. The problem number under each blank tells you where to look in Section 1. Write the letter of your answer from Section 1 on the blank.

__A__ __N__ __Y__   __N__ __U__ __M__ __B__ __E__ __R__
3.   5.   7.   5.   6.   1.   4.   2.   8.

__T__ __I__ __M__ __E__ __S__   __Z__ __E__ __R__ __O__
10. 9.   1.   2.   11.   12. 2.   8.   13.

__E__ __Q__ __U__ __A__ __L__ __S__   __Z__ __E__ __R__ __O__ .
2.   14. 6.   3.   15. 11.   12. 2.   8.   13.

The Array Game

Play alone or with a partner.

Materials: 10 × 10 grid for each player, two number cubes labeled 1–6, crayons or colored pencils

How to Play:

• Roll the number cubes. If you are playing with a partner, take turns rolling.

• Shade an array on your grid with a length and width that correspond to the numbers you rolled.

Example: Suppose you roll and .

Shade an array that is 2 squares wide and 6 squares long or 6 squares wide and 2 squares long. You may place the array anywhere on your grid. Arrays cannot overlap.

 or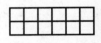

• The object of the game is to shade as much of the grid as possible during the time that you have to play the game.

Score: Your score is the total number of squares that you have shaded when time runs out.

Game 1

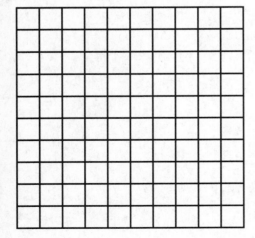

Game 2

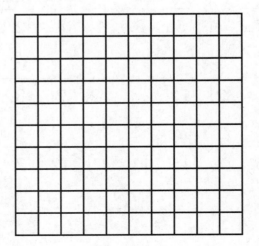

Score is _____

Score is _____

Number Patterns

A **multiple** is a number that is the product of a given number and another whole number. Some of the multiples of 3 are: 3, 6, 9, and 12.

1. On the number chart below, put a triangle around the numbers that are multiples of 4.
   Check students' charts.

2. Circle all the numbers that are multiples of 6.
   Check students' charts.

3. Shade all the numbers that are multiples of 8.
   Check students' charts.

4. List the numbers that have triangles around them and are also circled and shaded. _____ 24, 48, 72 _____

5. Are there any shaded numbers that do not have triangles around them? _____ no _____

1	2	3	4	5	6	7	8	9	10
11	12	13	14	15	16	17	18	19	20
21	22	23	24	25	26	27	28	29	30
31	32	33	34	35	36	37	38	39	40
41	42	43	44	45	46	47	48	49	50
51	52	53	54	55	56	57	58	59	60
61	62	63	64	65	66	67	68	69	70
71	72	73	74	75	76	77	78	79	80

Complete the number sentences.

6. __3__ × 8 = 24   7. __6__ × 8 = 48   8. __4__ × 8 = 32

9. __4__ × 6 = 24   10. __8__ × 6 = 48   11. __5__ × 6 = 30

Square Time

A **square array** is an array that is the same number of squares long as it is wide.

Complete the table, listing the sizes and products of some square arrays.

Square Arrays		
Length	Width	Total Squares
1	1	1
2	2	4
3	3	9
4	4	16
5	5	25
6	6	36
7	7	49
8	8	64

Use the table to solve. See students' work.

1. Jay and Barb each made a square array. Barb used more squares than Jay. Together they used 100 squares. How big was each array?

Jay's was 6 × 6;

Barb's was 8 × 8.

2. Tim, Mark, Dave, and Paul each made a square array. Together they used 100 squares. How big was each array?

Possible answer: Each made

a 5 × 5 square.

3. Sharon, Gayle, Joy, and Bev each made a square array. Joy and Bev used 22 more squares than Sharon and Gayle. Altogether the 4 girls used 122 squares. How big was each array?

Joy and Bev each made a 6 × 6 array;

Sharon and Gayle each made a 5 × 5 array.

Finding Factor Pairs

What kind of fruit is always grumpy?

To find out, draw a line to match each clue to the correct factor pair. Write the factor pair's code letter above the clue number at the bottom of page.

Factor Pairs	Code Letter
4,6	A
6,7	P
4,8	S
5,6	C
4,7	A
7,9	R
7,8	L
3,7	E
6,6	P
6,8	B

1. Their product is equal to 15 + 15.

2. Their product is odd.
   Their difference is 2.

3. Their product is equal to 3 × 8.

4. Their product is between 40 and 50.
   Their sum is even.

5. Their product is equal to 14 + 14.

6. Their product is about 40.
   Their difference is 1.

7. Their product is between 35 and 40.

8. Their product is greater than 50.
   Their difference is 1.

9. Their product is equal to 28 − 7.

10. Their product is even.
    Their difference is 4.

C R A B   A P P L E S
___ ___ ___ ___   ___ ___ ___ ___ ___ ___
1.   2.   3.   4.   5.   6.   7.   8.   9.   10.

Row after Row

Sam displays his apples in rows in his supermarket.

- Circle two fact arrays in each display of apples.
- Write the facts you used to find the total number of apples. Check students' arrays. Possible answers are given.

1.

   3 × 4 = 12; 3 × 8 = 24;

   12 + 24 = 36; there are

   36 apples.

2.

   4 × 7 = 28; 4 × 4 = 16;

   28 + 16 = 44; there are

   44 apples.

3.

   3 × 6 = 18; 3 × 6 = 18;

   18 + 18 = 36; there are

   36 apples.

4.

   4 × 6 = 24; 4 × 6 = 24;

   24 + 24 = 48; there are

   48 apples.

5.

   5 × 8 = 40; 5 × 4 = 20;

   40 + 20 = 60; there are

   60 apples.

6.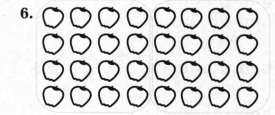

   4 × 4 = 16; 4 × 4 = 16;

   16 + 16 = 32; there are

   32 apples.

Combination Challenge

Use the numbers and symbols in each circle to make
4 different number sentences. Each number and symbol
can be used only once in a sentence, but they can be
used in more than one sentence. The first problem is
done for you. Possible answers are given. Check
students' sentences.

1. $3 \times 9 = 27$

$3 \times 4 = 12$

$3 \times 7 = 21$

$2 \times 7 = 14$

Circle: 3 9 / 1 × = 4 / 2 7

2. $0 \times 4 = 0$

$4 \times 4 = 16$

$10 \times 4 = 40$

$1 \times 4 = 4$

Circle: 0 4 / 1 × = 0 / 4 6

3. $1 \times 9 = 9$

$0 \times 9 = 0$

$9 \times 9 = 81$

$10 \times 9 = 90$

Circle: 9 0 / 1 × = 0 / 8 9

4. $4 \times 9 = 36$

$7 \times 9 = 63$

$7 \times 7 = 49$

$6 \times 9 = 54$

Circle: 7 5 9 / 6 × = 4 / 3 7

5. $2 \times 9 = 18$

$8 \times 9 = 72$

$7 \times 2 = 14$

$8 \times 2 = 16$

Circle: 2 9 / 1 × = 8 / 4 6 7

6. $7 \times 9 = 63$

$6 \times 9 = 54$

$8 \times 7 = 56$

$4 \times 9 = 36$

Circle: 7 9 / 6 × = 4 / 5 8 3

7. $5 \times 9 = 45$

$10 \times 4 = 40$

$10 \times 5 = 50$

$5 \times 1 = 5$

Circle: 5 0 9 / 1 × = 4 / 5 0 4

8. $8 \times 8 = 64$

$8 \times 6 = 48$

$10 \times 6 = 60$

$10 \times 8 = 80$

Circle: 0 8 1 / 6 × = 6 / 8 4 0

What's the Rule?

Ken and Mary are playing a game. First Mary draws a design and then Ken thinks of a rule and draws his design. When the table is completed, Mary tries to guess the rule Ken followed. They change roles and play again. Help Mary and Ken find the rules. Designs may vary. Check rules.

Mary	⬜⬜	⬜⬜⬜	⬜⬜⬜⬜	⬜⬜⬜⬜⬜	⬜⬜⬜⬜⬜⬜
Ken					

Rule: Multiply the number of squares in Mary's design by 3.

Ken					
Mary					

Rule: Multiply the number of lines in Ken's design by 2.

Choose a partner and play Mary and Ken's game. Designs will vary.

Your Name ____				
Your partner's name ____				

Rule: Answers will vary.

Missing Factors

Here are some Multiplication Squares to challenge
your multiplication skills! Fill in the missing factors
to complete the squares. Possible answers are given.

1.

×	3	5	9
2 × 4	24	40	72
3 × 3	27	45	81
5 × 2	30	50	90

2.

×	4	10	7
2 × 3	24	60	42
3 × 3	36	90	63
8 × 0	0	0	0

3.

×	2	8	9
2 × 5	20	80	90
1 × 7	14	56	63
3 × 3	18	72	81

4.

×	6	8	3
2 × 2	24	32	12
3 × 2	36	48	18
9 × 1	54	72	27

5.

×	6	4	0
3 × 3	54	36	0
7 × 1	42	28	0
2 × 2	24	16	0

6.

×	10	8	6
3 × 3	90	72	54
1 × 5	50	40	30
4 × 2	80	64	48

7.

×	2	4	5
9 × 1	18	36	45
1 × 7	14	28	35
2 × 5	20	40	50

8.

×	2	4	6
2 × 2	8	16	24
1 × 5	10	20	30
2 × 3	12	24	36

Name _____

Property Match Game

Play with a partner.

Materials: Expression cards shown below; scissors

How to Play:
- Cut apart the expression cards and place them facedown on a table.
- Players take turns. Turn over two cards. Determine whether the cards are an example of a multiplication property. If so, name the property. If not, place the cards back on the table facedown.
- If the property is named correctly, keep the cards. If not, place the cards back on the table facedown.
- When all the cards have been picked up, the player with more cards wins the game!

5 × 6	(2 × 2) + (2 × 7)	7
2 × 9	0 × 7	8 × (4 × 2)
9 × 1	(7 × 2) × 5	(3 × 2) × 4
0	(4 × 5) + (4 × 3)	6 × 5
(8 × 4) × 2	7 × (2 × 5)	7 × 1
3 × (2 × 4)	1 × 9	4 × 8

Make up your own set of cards. Trade with another pair of classmates, and play again.

CW60   Challenge

Name _____

Special Delivery

In each problem, the mailboxes have the same number of letters inside. Write the total number of letters for each problem.

1. ⬜ + ⬜ + ⬜ + ✉ ✉

Key: ⬜ = 5 letters

17 letters

2. ⬜ + ⬜ + ⬜ + ✉ ✉ ✉ ✉

Key: ⬜ = 10 letters

34 letters

3. ⬜ + ⬜ + ⬜ + ⬜ + ✉ ✉ ✉ ✉ ✉ ✉ ✉

Key: ⬜ = 8 letters

39 letters

4. ⬜ + ⬜ + ⬜ − ✉ ✉

Key: ⬜ = 9 letters

25 letters

5. ⬜ + ⬜ + ✉ ✉ ✉ ✉ ✉ ✉

Key: ⬜ = 7 letters

20 letters

6. ⬜ + ⬜ + ⬜ + ⬜ + ⬜ + ⬜ − ✉ ✉ ✉

Key: ⬜ = 9 letters

51 letters

7. 4 × ⬜ + ✉ ✉

Key: ⬜ = 3 letters

14 letters

8. 3 × ⬜ + ✉ ✉ ✉ ✉

Key: ⬜ = 8 letters

28 letters

9. 6 × ⬜ − ✉ ✉ ✉

Key: ⬜ = 5 letters

27 letters

10. 8 × ⬜ + ✉ ✉ ✉ ✉ ✉

Key: ⬜ = 9 letters

77 letters

Challenge CW61

Paintbrush Division

The jars in each row need to be filled with the same number of paintbrushes. Draw the paintbrushes in each jar and complete the number sentence. Check students' drawings.

1.

Total number of paintbrushes: 12

Paintbrushes in each jar: __4__

$12 \div 3 =$ __4__

2.

Total number of paintbrushes: 8

Paintbrushes in each jar: __2__

$8 \div 4 =$ __2__

3.

Total number of paintbrushes: 12

Paintbrushes in each jar: __6__

$12 \div 2 =$ __6__

4.

Total number of paintbrushes: 15

Paintbrushes in each jar: __3__

$15 \div 5 =$ __3__

5.

Total number of paintbrushes: 18

Paintbrushes in each jar: __6__

$18 \div 3 =$ __6__

6.

Total number of paintbrushes: 20

Paintbrushes in each jar: __5__

$20 \div 4 =$ __5__

Complete the chart.

	Number of Paintbrushes	Number of Jars	Number of Paintbrushes in Each Jar
7.	24	4	6
8.	21	3	7
9.	30	5	6

Animal Division

Separate the animals into groups. Draw a circle around each group. Then complete the number sentence. Check students' work.

1. 4 cats in each group

$8 \div 4 =$ ___2___

2. 3 dogs in each group

$9 \div 3 =$ ___3___

3. 3 birds in each group

$12 \div 3 =$ ___4___

4. 5 turtles in each group

$10 \div 5 =$ ___2___

5. 5 mice in each group

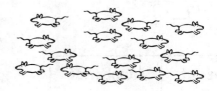

$15 \div 5 =$ ___3___

6. 3 fish in each group

$18 \div 3 =$ ___6___

Complete the chart.

	Number of Animals	Number in Each Group	Number of Equal Groups
7.	18 puppies	3	6
8.	20 kittens	4	5
9.	24 gerbils	6	4
10.	30 guinea pigs	5	6

Missing Numbers

Complete each table.

1.

Number of Students	Number of Hands
1	2
4	8
6	12
2	4
9	18
7	14
5	10

2.

Number of Tricycles	Number of Wheels
1	3
3	9
7	21
6	18
9	27
4	12
8	24

3.

Number of 4-Leaf Clovers	Number of Leaves
1	4
3	12
5	20
4	16
9	36
2	8
8	32

4.

Number of Ants	Number of Legs
1	6
2	12
5	30
3	18
4	24
7	42
8	48

Fact Family Patterns

1. Fill in the missing numbers in the first three rows of
   the Fact Table to complete each number sentence.

Fact Table			
Blue 18 ÷ 2 = _9_	Red 3 × 6 = _18_	Green 24 ÷ 8 = _3_	Yellow 6 × 4 = _24_
Red 6 × _3_ = 18	Green 24 ÷ 3 = _8_	Yellow 4 × _6_ = 24	Blue 9 × _2_ = 18
Green 3 × _8_ = 24	Yellow 24 ÷ _4_ = 6	Blue 2 × _9_ = 18	Red 18 ÷ 6 = _3_
Yellow 24 ÷ 6 = 4	Blue 18 ÷ 9 = 2	Red 18 ÷ 3 = 6	Green 8 × 3 = 24

2. Use the colors shown below to color all the facts in
   the Fact Table above that belong to each fact family.
   Check students' work.

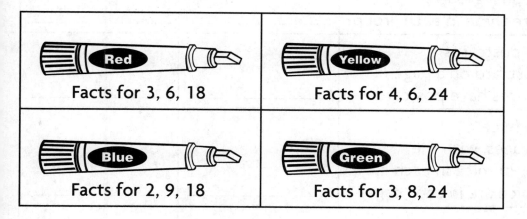

Red Facts for 3, 6, 18	**Yellow** Facts for 4, 6, 24
Blue Facts for 2, 9, 18	**Green** Facts for 3, 8, 24

3. Notice the color pattern in the Fact Table, and
   notice that each fact family is missing a fact. Write
   the missing fact from each fact family in the bottom
   row of the Fact Table. Arrange the facts so that the
   color pattern continues.

Number Sentences

Complete the division and multiplication sentences that
solve each problem.

Problem	Division Sentence	Multiplication Sentence
1. There are 12 kittens. There are 3 kittens in each basket. How many baskets are there in all?	12 ÷ 3 = ___4___	___4___ × 3 = 12
2. There are 15 chairs. There are 5 equal rows of chairs. How many chairs are there in each row?	15 ÷ 5 = ___3___	5 × ___3___ = 15

Write a division sentence that can be used to solve each
problem. Then write a related multiplication sentence.

Problem	Division Sentence	Multiplication Sentence
3. There are 21 children. There are 3 equal groups. How many are there in each group?	21 ÷ 3 = 7	3 × 7 = 21
4. There are 15 postcards. There is 1 postcard on a page. How many pages have postcards?	15 ÷ 1 = 15	1 × 15 = 15
5. There are 20 mice. There are 4 cages, with the same number of mice in each cage. How many mice are in each cage?	20 ÷ 4 = 5	4 × 5 = 20
6. There are 24 wheels. How many cars are there?	24 ÷ 4 = 6	6 × 4 = 24
7. There are 16 eyes. How many people are there?	16 ÷ 2 = 8	8 × 2 = 16

Favorite Numbers

Karen, Tyler, and Daniela are friends who have made
posters of their favorite numbers. Think about each
of their favorite numbers and then answer the
questions below.

1. Which friends have favorite numbers that can all
   be divided by 2?

   Karen and Tyler

2. Which friends have favorite numbers that can all
   be divided by 5?

   Daniela and Tyler

3. Which friend has favorite numbers that can all be
   divided by both 2 and 5?

   Tyler

4. What else do Karen's favorite numbers have
   in common?

   Possible answer: They are all even numbers.

5. What else do Daniela's favorite numbers have
   in common?

   Possible answer: The ones digits are either 0 or 5.

The Same and Different

Divide. In each row, circle the problem that is different
from the other problems in that row. Explain how the
remaining problems are alike.

Answers may vary. Possible answers are given.

1. $24 \div 3 =$ __8__   2. $40 \div 4 =$ __10__   3. $15 \div 3 =$ __5__

quotients are even numbers

4. $36 \div 4 =$ __9__   5. $32 \div 4 =$ __8__   6. $18 \div 3 =$ __6__

quotients are even numbers

7. $20 \div 4 =$ __5__   8. $21 \div 3 =$ __7__   9. $12 \div 3 =$ __4__

quotients are odd numbers

10. $16 \div 4 =$ __4__   11. $9 \div 3 =$ __3__   12. $6 \div 3 =$ __2__

quotient is same as divisor

13. $30 \div 3 =$ __10__   14. $8 \div 4 =$ __2__   15. $20 \div 4 =$ __5__

quotients are divisible by 5

16. Write two division problems that are alike in some
way and one division problem that is different in
some way. Have a classmate solve your problems
and tell which two problems are alike and why.

___ ÷ ___ = ___   ___ ÷ ___ = ___   ___ ÷ ___ = ___

Check students' work.

_____

_____

_____

_____

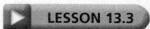
Writing Equations

In each table below, the numbers in the ☐ column are dividends. The numbers in the △ column are quotients. Find the divisor that works for each table. Then, write the equation below the table, and complete the table. The first equation has been written for you.

1.

☐	△
4	2
8	4
0	0
6	3
10	5
20	10
14	7

Equation:

$$☐ \div 2 = △$$

2.

☐	△
15	3
35	7
10	2
25	5
5	1
0	0
45	9

Equation:

$$☐ \div 5 = △$$

3.

☐	△
20	5
16	4
4	1
12	3
8	2
36	9
0	0

Equation:

$$☐ \div 4 = △$$

4.

☐	△
12	2
24	4
6	1
30	5
42	7
0	0
18	3

Equation:

$$☐ \div 6 = △$$

5.

☐	△
12	4
27	9
6	2
3	1
0	0
18	6
9	3

Equation:

$$☐ \div 3 = △$$

6.

☐	△
4	4
8	8
7	7
5	5
0	0
3	3
2	2

Equation:

$$☐ \div 1 = △$$

Write a Problem

Write an expression that describes each picture. Then write
a word problem to go with the picture and the expression.
Answers may vary. Possible answers are given.

1.

Expression: _____ 8 ÷ 2 _____

The Problem

A pet store has 8 kittens. It

keeps an equal number of

kittens in each of two cages.

How many kittens are in each

cage?

2.

Expression: _____ 6 + 5 _____

The Problem

Six birds are sitting in a tree.

Five more birds join them.

How many birds are in the tree

now?

3.

Expression: _____ 9 − 3 _____

The Problem

The boy had 9 balloons. Three

of the balloons blew away. How

many balloons does he have now?

4.

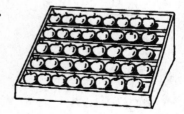

Expression: _____ 5 × 8 _____

The Problem

The grocery store displays

apples in 5 equal rows of

8 apples. How many apples are

in the display?

Solving Problems at the Aquarium

Aquarium	Admission	Sea Lion Show
	$6 adults $4 children under 12 $45 Family membership— free admission for one year	10:30, 12:00, 1:30, 3:00

1. Mr. and Mrs. Young and their 6-year-old triplets go to the aquarium. How much do they pay?

   $24.00 (or $45 for 1 yr. membership)

2. The sea lion show lasts 45 minutes. How much time is there between shows?

   45 min

3. The theater where the sea lions perform can seat 600 people. There are 475 people sitting in the theater for the 12:00 show. How many more people can be seated before the theater is full?

   125 more people

4. Mr. Ruiz buys a family membership. He goes to the aquarium with his 4-year-old son 6 times during the year. How much money does he save?

   $15.00

5. A class of 24 students visits the aquarium. They divide into 4 groups. How many students are in each group?

   6 students

6. John buys a book about sharks for $4.95 and a shell for $1.35. How much money does he spend?

   $6.30

7. Meg counts 12 starfish and 9 hermit crabs in a display. How many more starfish are there than hermit crabs?

   3 more starfish

8. Jesse learned that a seahorse egg hatches in 50 to 60 days. About how many weeks is this?

   about 8 weeks

Fun with Facts

Follow the arrows to solve each problem. Write
the answer inside the empty box. You may use a
multiplication table to help you multiply and divide.

1. $\boxed{36} \rightarrow \boxed{\div 6} \rightarrow \boxed{\times 4} \rightarrow \boxed{\div 8} \rightarrow \boxed{3}$

2. $\boxed{48} \rightarrow \boxed{\div 8} \rightarrow \boxed{+15} \rightarrow \boxed{\div 7} \rightarrow \boxed{3}$

3. $\boxed{63} \rightarrow \boxed{\div 7} \rightarrow \boxed{\times 2} \rightarrow \boxed{\div 6} \rightarrow \boxed{3}$

4. $\boxed{56} \rightarrow \boxed{\div 7} \rightarrow \boxed{-2} \rightarrow \boxed{\div 6} \rightarrow \boxed{1}$

5. $\boxed{35} \rightarrow \boxed{\div 7} \rightarrow \boxed{+27} \rightarrow \boxed{\div 8} \rightarrow \boxed{4}$

6. $\boxed{16} \rightarrow \boxed{\div 8} \rightarrow \boxed{\times 6} \rightarrow \boxed{-4} \rightarrow \boxed{8}$

7. $\boxed{8} \rightarrow \boxed{\times 3} \rightarrow \boxed{\div 6} \rightarrow \boxed{+4} \rightarrow \boxed{8}$

Write an operation and a number in the empty box.

8. $\boxed{72} \rightarrow \boxed{\div 8} \rightarrow \boxed{\div 3} \rightarrow \boxed{\times 7} \rightarrow \boxed{21}$
   or $+18$

9. $\boxed{24} \rightarrow \boxed{\div 6} \rightarrow \boxed{\times 9} \rightarrow \boxed{\div 6} \rightarrow \boxed{6}$
   or -30

10. $\boxed{8} \rightarrow \boxed{\times 8} \rightarrow \boxed{-8} \rightarrow \boxed{\div 7} \rightarrow \boxed{8}$
    or -48

Make up your own problems. Use at least one multiplication
or division step in each. Check students' work. Answers will vary.

11. $\boxed{} \rightarrow \boxed{} \rightarrow \boxed{} \rightarrow \boxed{} \rightarrow \boxed{}$

12. $\boxed{} \rightarrow \boxed{} \rightarrow \boxed{} \rightarrow \boxed{} \rightarrow \boxed{}$

Name _____

Divide by 9 and 10

Divide. Connect the dots in order from least to
greatest quotient.

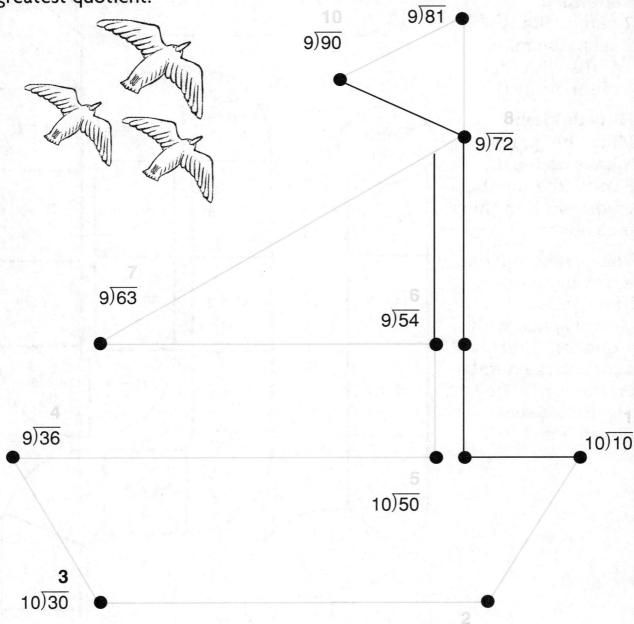

9)81

10   9)90

9

8   9)72

7   9)63

6   9)54

4   9)36

1   10)10

5   10)50

3   10)30

2   9)18

On grid paper, design your own connect-the-dots picture
using the division facts you know. Have a friend solve.

Challenge   CW73

The Quotient Game

Play with a partner.

Materials:
2 game tokens
2 sets of number cards with the numbers 1–10

How to Play:
Place the game tokens on **Start**. Shuffle the number cards and turn them face down.

Take turns drawing a number card. Move forward to the closest space with a quotient that matches the number on the card. The first player to reach **Finish** wins!

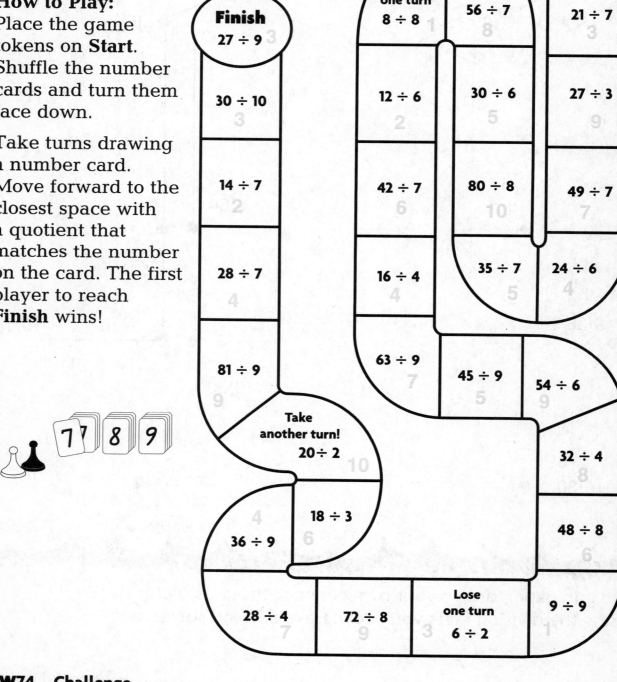

What's the Cost?

Complete the table and solve each problem.

1. Mr. Brown pays $3 for 1 bag of dog food. How much will he pay for 4 bags of food?

Bags	1	2	3	4	5
Cost	$3	$6	$9	$12	$15

$12

2. In Jill's class, 5 students paid a total of $25 for a field trip. If each student pays an equal amount, how much will 3 students pay?

Students	1	2	3	4	5
Cost	$5	$10	$15	$20	$25

$15

3. During the summer, Liza earns $6 every 2 days walking her neighbor's pets. How much does she earn in 5 days?

Days	1	2	3	4	5
Earns	$3	$6	$9	$12	$15

$15

4. It costs $16 for every 4 times the Moran family goes swimming at the pool. If the cost of each visit remains the same, how much will it cost for the Morans to go to the pool 10 times?

Times	1	2	3	4	5
Cost	$4	$8	$12	$16	$20

Times	6	7	8	9	10
Cost	$24	$28	$32	$36	$40

$40

5. A student can buy 9 lunch tokens for $18. If the cost of each token remains the same, how much will a student pay for 3 lunch tokens? How much will 10 lunch tokens cost?

Tokens	1	2	3	4	5
Cost	$2	$4	$6	$8	$10

Tokens	6	7	8	9	10
Cost	$12	$14	$16	$18	$20

$6; $20

What Number Am I?

Read each number riddle. Use the clues to identify each number.

1. If you add 7 to me and then divide the result by me, the answer is 8. What number am I?

_____ 1

2. Multiply me by 5, and you get a number that is 5 more than 20. What number am I?

_____ 5

3. Divide me by 3, or multiply me by 6. The answer will be the same. What number am I?

_____ 0

4. When you multiply me by myself, you get me again! What number am I?

_____ 1 or 0

5. Divide 12 by 3, and you get me. Divide 12 by me, and you get 3. What number am I?

_____ 4

6. If you multiply any number by me, the sum of the digits in the product equals me. What number am I?

_____ 9

7. If you divide 30 by me, the answer is 3 doubled. What number am I?

_____ 5

8. If you divide any number by me, your answer will be that number again! What number am I?

_____ 1

9. Write your own number riddle. After solving it yourself, ask a classmate to try it.

_____ Answers will vary.

_____

_____

Name _____

Sara's System

Sara collects dolls from around the world. The table shows what kinds of dolls she has in her collection.

SARA'S DOLLS			
Number	**Country**	**Gender**	**Adult or Child**
2	Australia	Male	Adult
3	Australia	Female	Adult
5	Australia	Female	Child
1	United States	Female	Adult
4	United States	Male	Child
5	United States	Female	Child
1	Sweden	Male	Adult
2	Japan	Male	Adult
3	Japan	Female	Adult
4	Japan	Male	Child
5	Mexico	Female	Child
3	Israel	Male	Adult
2	Israel	Female	Child

Sara sorted her dolls into four boxes. All the dolls in each box have two things in common. Write what type of doll is in each box.

Male Adults = 8; Female Adults = 7; Male Children = 8;

Female Children = 17

You Decide

You work at a grocery store.

You must decide what brand of crackers to order.

A survey is conducted to help you.

Think about the price of the crackers and the number of votes when you decide.

CRACKERS		
Brand of Crackers	**Number of Votes**	**Price per Bag**
Wavy	23	30¢
Light 'n' Salty	13	36¢
Crispy Crunchies	45	27¢
Toasties	22	20¢
Frickles	61	23¢
Ring-a-Ling	48	18¢
Goodies	27	25¢

Examine the table. Pick three brands to order.
Explain your decision.

Possible answers: I would stock Frickles, Crispy Crunchies, and

Goodies because they are priced in the middle and had

a large number of votes. I think the names are fun.

You Group

The first table shows one way to group the shapes below.
Find another way to group the shapes. Then make a table
to show the other way.

NUMBER OF LINES			
	One Line	Two Lines	Four Lines
Circles	7	6	7
Triangles	3	6	5

Possible answers are shown.

DIRECTION OF LINES				
	Horizontal Lines	Vertical Lines	Diagonal Lines	All Three Lines
Circles	6	6	6	2
Triangles	4	5	3	2

Spinning

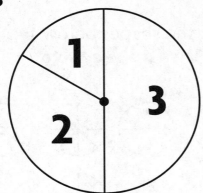 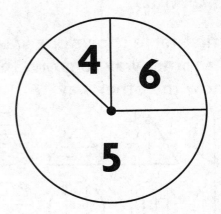

Use a paper clip and a pencil.

Put your pencil in the paper clip to hold the paper clip in the center point of the circle. Spin the paper clip on each spinner.

In the table, record the sum of the two numbers you spin. Repeat this 50 times. Tallies will vary. Possible answers are given.

1. Which sum happened the most?

   _____The sum of 8 happened_____

   _____the most._____

2. Which sum happened the least?

   _____The sum of 5 happened_____

   _____the least._____

SPINNER SUMS	
Sum	Tally
5	
6	
7	
8	
9	

3. Which two sums do you think should happen more times?

   Possible answer: 7 and 8, since the sections for 2, 3, and 5 are

   _____larger than the other sections on the spinners._____

   _____

Name _____

What's in a Name?

Jennifer is comparing the number of letters in her
classmates' first names. She printed each student's name
on a piece of paper. She then began to count and record
the number of letters in each name.

1. Complete Jennifer's line plot by recording the number of
   letters in the first names of the students in her class.

Jennifer	Zachary	Lee	Elizabeth	Dimitri
Ted	Juan	Trudi	Malcolm	Chiang
Carl	Paul	Courtney	Kevin	Alan

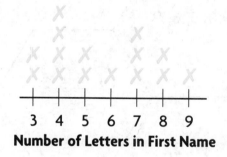

3 4 5 6 7 8 9
Number of Letters in First Name

For 2–5, use the completed line plot.

2. How many students have 7 letters in their first name?

   ___3 students___

3. What is the mode for the number of letters for a first
   name in Jennifer's class?

   ___4 letters___

4. What is the range in this data?

   ___6 letters___

5. Would the data be different if you
   made a line plot for the number of
   letters in the first names of students
   in your class? Make a list of names
   and show the data in a line plot.

   ___Yes; Check students' work.___

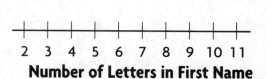

2 3 4 5 6 7 8 9 10 11
Number of Letters in First Name

Mean and Median Pathway

Find the mean and median for each of the following sets of numbers. Then, find and color the sets of numbers whose mean and median are equal. Find a path from Start to Finish.

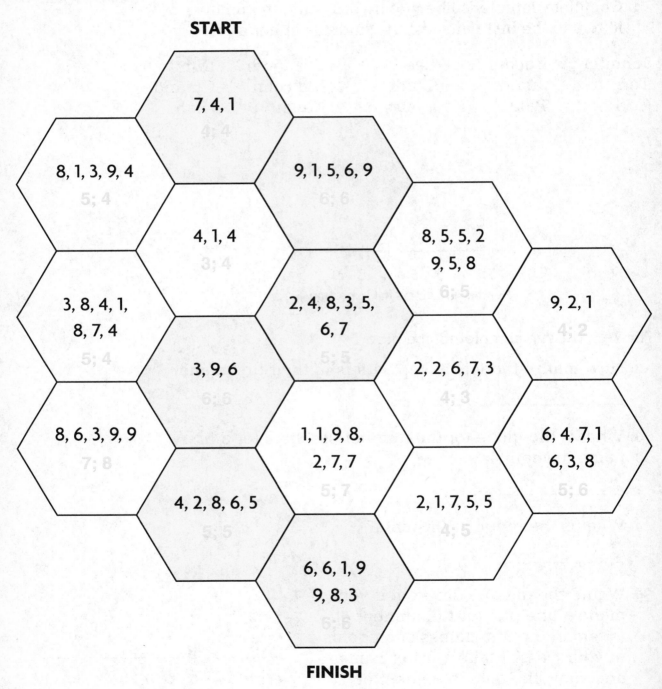

START

7, 4, 1
4; 4

8, 1, 3, 9, 4
5; 4

9, 1, 5, 6, 9
6; 6

4, 1, 4
3; 4

8, 5, 5, 2
9, 5, 8
6; 5

3, 8, 4, 1,
8, 7, 4
5; 4

2, 4, 8, 3, 5,
6, 7
5; 5

9, 2, 1
4; 2

3, 9, 6
6; 6

2, 2, 6, 7, 3
4; 3

8, 6, 3, 9, 9
7; 8

1, 1, 9, 8,
2, 7, 7
5; 7

6, 4, 7, 1
6, 3, 8
5; 6

4, 2, 8, 6, 5
5; 5

2, 1, 7, 5, 5
4; 5

6, 6, 1, 9
9, 8, 3
6; 6

FINISH

Parts of a Picture

The pictograph shows the number of students in seven third-grade classes.

	Third-Grade Classes
Mr. Jones	○○○○○○○○
Mrs. Smith	○○○○○○◖
Mr. Flores	○○○○○○○
Mr. Brown	○○○○○○○○○◖
Ms. Tanaka	○○○○○○
Mrs. Hanson	○○○○○○○○◹
Mrs. Wright	○○○○○○○◖

Key: Each ○ = 4 students.

1. Each ○ equals how many students?

   4 students
   _____

2. Each ◖ equals how many students? Explain.

   2 students; it is only half of a symbol. Half of 4 is 2.
   _____

   _____

3. Each ◹ equals how many students? Explain.

   1 student; it is only one fourth of a symbol.
   _____

   One fourth of 4 is 1.
   _____

4. List the number of students each teacher has in order from most students to fewest students.

   Mr. Brown, 38; Mrs. Hanson, 33; Mr. Jones, 32; Mrs. Wright, 30;
   _____

   Mr. Flores, 28; Mrs. Smith, 26; Ms. Tanaka, 24
   _____

Name _____

What Is Left?

Starting with 2, put a diagonal line from upper left to lower right through every second number.

Starting with 3, put a diagonal line from lower left to upper right through every third number.

Starting with 5, put a vertical line through every fifth number.

Starting with 7, put a horizontal line through every seventh number.

1	2	3	4	5	6	7	8	9	10
11	12	13	14	15	16	17	18	19	20
21	22	23	24	25	26	27	28	29	30
31	32	33	34	35	36	37	38	39	40
41	42	43	44	45	46	47	48	49	50
51	52	53	54	55	56	57	58	59	60
61	62	63	64	65	66	67	68	69	70
71	72	73	74	75	76	77	78	79	80
81	82	83	84	85	86	87	88	89	90
91	92	93	94	95	96	97	98	99	100

1. Circle any numbers not marked. What numbers are circled?

1, 11, 13, 17, 19, 23, 29, 31, 37, 41, 43, 47, 53, 59, 61, 67, 71, 73,

79, 83, 89, 97

2. Which numbers have all four types of lines drawn through them?

none of them

Pay Up

Mr. Santos rewards his students for doing their homework. Each time they do a homework assignment, he gives them a smiling face sticker. When students have collected 8 smiling face stickers, they receive a pencil.

Complete the chart for each student.

Name	Stickers	Number of Pencils	Stickers Left Over
Sylvia	☺☺☺☺☺☺☺	0	7
Joshua	☺☺☺☺☺☺☺☺☺☺☺☺☺☺☺	1	7
Hidori	☺☺☺☺☺☺☺☺☺☺☺ ☺☺☺☺☺☺☺☺☺☺☺	2	6
Brandon	☺☺☺☺☺☺☺☺☺☺☺ ☺☺☺☺☺	2	0
Jessica	☺☺☺☺☺☺☺☺☺☺☺☺	1	4
Martha	☺☺☺☺☺☺☺☺☺☺☺☺☺☺ ☺☺☺☺☺☺☺☺☺☺☺☺☺☺	3	4
Tiffany	☺☺☺☺☺☺☺☺☺☺	1	2
George	☺☺☺	0	3
Tony	☺☺☺☺☺☺☺☺☺☺☺☺ ☺☺☺☺☺☺☺☺☺☺☺	2	7
Justin	☺☺☺☺☺☺☺☺☺☺☺☺☺☺	1	6
Paola	☺☺☺☺☺☺☺☺☺☺☺ ☺☺☺☺☺☺☺☺☺☺☺ ☺☺☺☺☺☺☺☺☺☺☺	4	1

1. Who received the most pencils? the fewest pencils?

   Paola; George and Sylvia

2. If they all decided to share, are there enough pencils? Explain.

   Everyone could have 1 pencil. There would be 6 left over.

Grocery List

Raul and Laurie are going grocery shopping. They have split the shopping list in half. Below is a map of the store showing where the items can be found. Tell what items Raul and Laurie buy.

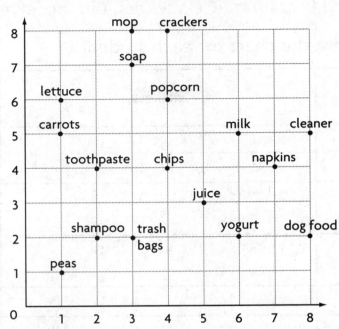

Laurie's list		Raul's list	
1. (1,1)	peas	(4,4)	chips
2. (3,7)	soap	(2,2)	shampoo
3. (8,2)	dog food	(7,4)	napkins
4. (5,3)	juice	(6,5)	milk
5. (3,2)	trash bags	(1,5)	carrots
6. (8,5)	cleaner	(4,8)	crackers
7. (6,2)	yogurt	(3,8)	mop
8. (1,6)	lettuce	(4,6)	popcorn

9. If Raul and Laurie go to (2,4), where do they meet?

_____ at the toothpaste _____

Connect the Dots

Follow these steps to make a line graph for the
data in the table.

Step 1 Look at the table to find the number
of sales for Monday. On the line
graph, find the line for Monday and
follow it up to the horizontal line for
that number.

Step 2 Place a point on the graph.

Step 3 Repeat Steps 1–2 for the other days.

Step 4 Use a ruler to connect the point for
Monday with the point for Tuesday.
Continue to connect the points until
all of the points are connected.

Book Fair Sales	
Day	Number of Books Sold
Monday	30
Tuesday	20
Wednesday	30
Thursday	45
Friday	40

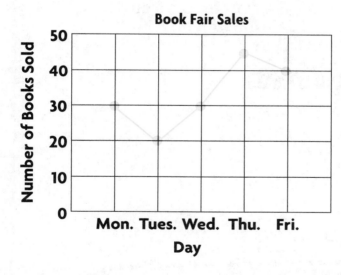

For 1–3, use the line graph.

1. On what day were there the
fewest sales? the most sales?

   ___Tuesday; Thursday___

2. On which days were there the
same number of sales?

   ___Monday and Wednesday___

3. What day had more sales than the day before it,
but had fewer sales than the day after it?

   ___Wednesday___

No Rulers Allowed!

Measure and cut a 5-inch strip and a 2-inch strip from a piece of paper.

5 inches

2 inches

Use the two strips to measure the drawings in Problems 1–4 to the nearest half inch. Do **not** use a ruler.

Hints:

* If you fold each strip in half, you will have two more measuring strips. Half of the 5-inch strip will be $2\frac{1}{2}$ inches long. Half of the 2-inch strip will be _____1 inch long_____.

* You can compare or combine the rulers to form different lengths.

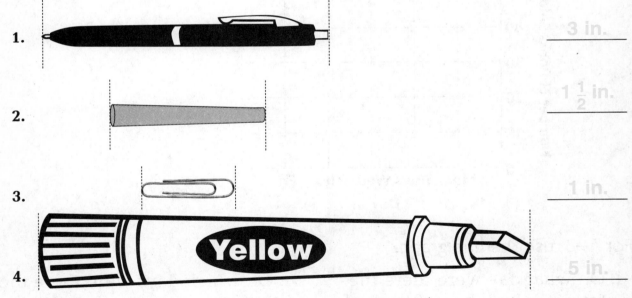

1. _____3 in._____

2. $1\frac{1}{2}$ in.

3. _____1 in._____

4. _____5 in._____

5. Tell how you measured the pen in Problem 1.

_____Possible answer: I used the 2-inch strip. Then I_____

_____folded the strip in half to make a 1-inch strip._____

_____The pen measured 3 inches._____

Name _____

Choose the Best Unit

1. What is the best unit for measuring each
   item on the quilt? Use the key to color
   each triangle on the quilt.
   Check students' work.

Key	
inch	red
foot or yard	yellow
mile	green

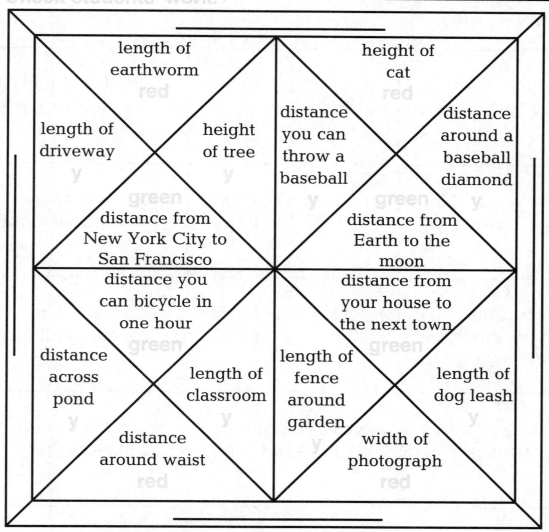

length of earthworm — red

height of cat — red

length of driveway — y

height of tree — y

green

distance you can throw a baseball — y

distance around a baseball diamond — y

green

distance from New York City to San Francisco

distance from Earth to the moon

distance you can bicycle in one hour — green

distance from your house to the next town — green

distance across pond — y

length of classroom — y

length of fence around garden — y

length of dog leash — y

distance around waist — red

width of photograph — red

2. In the top border of the quilt, write the name of an item to
   be measured in feet or yards. Color the top border yellow.
   Answers will vary. Check students' answers.

3. In the bottom border of the quilt, write the name of an
   item to be measured in miles. Color the bottom border
   green. Answers will vary. Check students' answers.

4. In each side border of the quilt, write the name of an
   item to be measured in inches. Color the side borders
   red. Answers will vary. Check students' answers.

Making Sense of Measurements

Each box below makes a statement about capacity. Circle
the letter in the box if the statement could be true. Form
the answer to the riddle by writing the circled letters in
order on the blanks.

1. A A punch bowl holds 10 gallons.	**2. Z** A medicine bottle holds less than 1 cup.	**3. O** A bathtub holds less than 3 quarts.
4. E A tea kettle holds about 1 quart.	**5. R** Beth drinks about 3 cups of milk a day.	**6. T** An eyedropper holds about 1 cup.
7. O Sam bought 2 quarts of ice cream for his party.	**8. S** John's mug holds about 1 quart.	**9. C** Mary and Liz shared a pint of juice.
10. R The sink holds 20 gallons of water.	**11. U** Mrs. Frank made 2 quarts of soup.	**12. E** A car's gas tank holds less than 1 gallon.
13. P Jane used 3 gallons of water to wash her lunch dishes.	**14. S** Mr. Green made punch with 2 quarts of juice and 1 pint of sherbet.	**15. T** Sam poured 1 quart of milk into his glass.

How many cups of water can a funnel hold?

Z E R O   C U P S
___ ___ ___ ___ ___ ___ ___ ___ ___

Name _____

Balancing Toys

For 1–6, use the pictures to complete the sentences.
Then use those sentences to answer problems 7–11.

1.

The whistle weighs ___less___ than the block.

2.

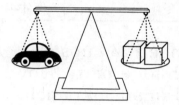

The car weighs ___more___ than the block.

3.

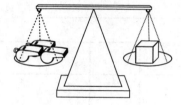

___3___ whistles weigh the same as 1 block.

4.

1 car weighs the same as ___2___ blocks.

5.

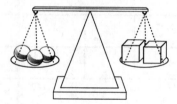

___3___ balls weigh the same as 2 blocks.

6.

1 pencil weighs ___less___ than the block.

7. How many whistles weigh the same as 1 car?

___6 whistles___

8. How many balls weigh the same as 1 car?

___3 balls___

A block weighs 3 ounces. Write the weight of the other toys.

9.

___1 ounce___

10.

___6 ounces___

11.

___2 ounces___

Challenge CW91

Name _____

How Much Do You Need?

Complete as much of each table as you need to solve each problem. Use the Table of Measures to help.

Table of Measures		
Length	**Capacity**	**Weight**
12 inches = 1 foot 3 feet = 1 yard	2 cups = 1 pint 4 cups = 1 quart 2 pints = 1 quart 8 pints = 1 gallon 4 quarts = 1 gallon	16 ounces = 1 pound

1. You need 24 cups of punch for a party. How many quarts of punch do you need?

Quarts	1	2	3	4	5	6
Cups	4	8	12	16	20	24

_____ 6 quarts

2. You need 32 ounces of meat for hamburgers. How many pounds of meat do you need?

Pounds	1	2				
Ounces	16	32				

_____ 2 pounds

3. You need 12 feet of ribbon to make a banner. How many yards of ribbon do you need?

Yards	1	2	3	4		
Feet	3	6	9	12		

_____ 4 yards

4. You take 20 quarts of water on a camping trip. How many gallon jugs do you carry?

Gallons	1	2	3	4	5	
Quarts	4	8	12	16	20	

_____ 5 gallon jugs

Estimated or Exact Relations

Complete each sentence. Circle *is about* or *equals* and write a whole number on the line. Use the Table of Measures for help.

Table of Measures		
Length	**Capacity**	**Weight**
12 inches = 1 foot 3 feet = 1 yard	2 cups = 1 pint 4 cups = 1 quart 2 pints = 1 quart 8 pints = 1 gallon 4 quarts = 1 gallon	16 ounces = 1 pound

1. 25 inches (is about / equals) ____2____ feet.

2. 2 gallons (is about / equals) ____8____ quarts.

3. 15 feet (is about / equals) ____5____ yards.

4. 7 pints (is about / equals) __3 or 4__ quarts.

5. 3 pounds (is about / equals) ____48____ ounces.

6. 20 feet (is about / equals) ____7____ yards.

7. 11 cups (is about / equals) __5 or 6__ pints.

8. 16 pints (is about / equals) ____2____ gallons.

9. 30 ounces (is about / equals) ____2____ pounds.

10. 5 gallons (is about / equals)____20____ quarts.

11. 23 cups (is about / equals) ____6____ quarts.

12. 48 inches (is about / equals) ____4____ feet.

Centimeter Estimation Game

Play with a partner.

Materials:

- table shown below for each player
- centimeter ruler

How to Play:

Step 1 Work with your partner to identify 10 objects or distances in the classroom that you will measure in centimeters. Record them in the first column of your tables.

Step 2 Work by yourself to estimate the length of each object or distance in centimeters. Record your estimates in the second column of your table.

Step 3 Work with your partner to measure the length of each object or distance to the nearest centimeter. Record these measurements in the third column of your tables.

Step 4 Work by yourself to find the difference between the estimated length and actual length of each object or distance. Record these differences in the fourth column of your table.

Step 5 Work by yourself to find the sum of the differences in the fourth column. The player with the lower sum wins!

Object/Distance	Estimated Length	Actual Length	Difference

What's the Order?

Order the lengths from least to greatest.

1. 305 cm, 31 km, 3 m, 35 dm

_____3 m, 305 cm, 35 dm, 31 km_____

2. 295 cm, 2 m, 2 km, 2 dm

_____2 dm, 2 m, 295 cm, 2 km_____

3. 15 km, 15 m, 15 dm, 51 cm

_____51 cm, 15 dm, 15 m, 15 km_____

4. 8 m, 878 cm, 78 m, 87 dm

_____8 m, 87 dm, 878 cm, 78 m_____

5. 355 cm, 5 m, 535 cm, 35 m

_____355 cm, 5 m, 535 cm, 35 m_____

6. 986 cm, 98 km, 86 m, 89 dm, 9 m

_____89 dm, 9 m, 986 cm, 86 m, 98 km_____

7. 92 km, 29 m, 92 dm, 290 cm, 229 dm

_____290 cm, 92 dm, 229 dm, 29 m, 92 km_____

8. Think of two times when metric units of length might be used.

_____Possible answers: in a science_____

_____class; in sports_____

9. Write a problem using the measurements listed in one of the problems above. Solve.

_____Check students' problems and solutions._____

_____

_____

Estimating and Comparing Capacity

Order the measurements from least to greatest capacity.

1. 5 L; 5,100 mL; 1,005 mL; 1 L

   _1 L; 1,005 mL; 5L; 5,100 mL_

2. 2,950 mL; 3,120 mL; 3 L; 21 L

   _2,950 mL; 3 L; 3,120 mL; 21 L_

3. 7,040 mL; 4,770 mL; 4 L; 7,400 mL

   _4 L; 4,770 mL; 7,040 mL; 7,400 mL_

4. 6,500 mL; 5 L; 5,600 mL; 6 L; 5,066 mL

   _5 L; 5,066 mL; 5,600 mL; 6 L; 6,500 mL_

5. List some containers that hold liquids. Record which metric unit would be better for measuring each container's capacity. Check students' tables.

Container	Milliliter (mL) or Liter (L)
Bottle of maple syrup	mL
Bottle of water	L

6. Write a problem using data from one of the problems above. Solve. Check students' problems and solutions.

_____

_____

Graphing Mass

The masses of five students are shown in the table.

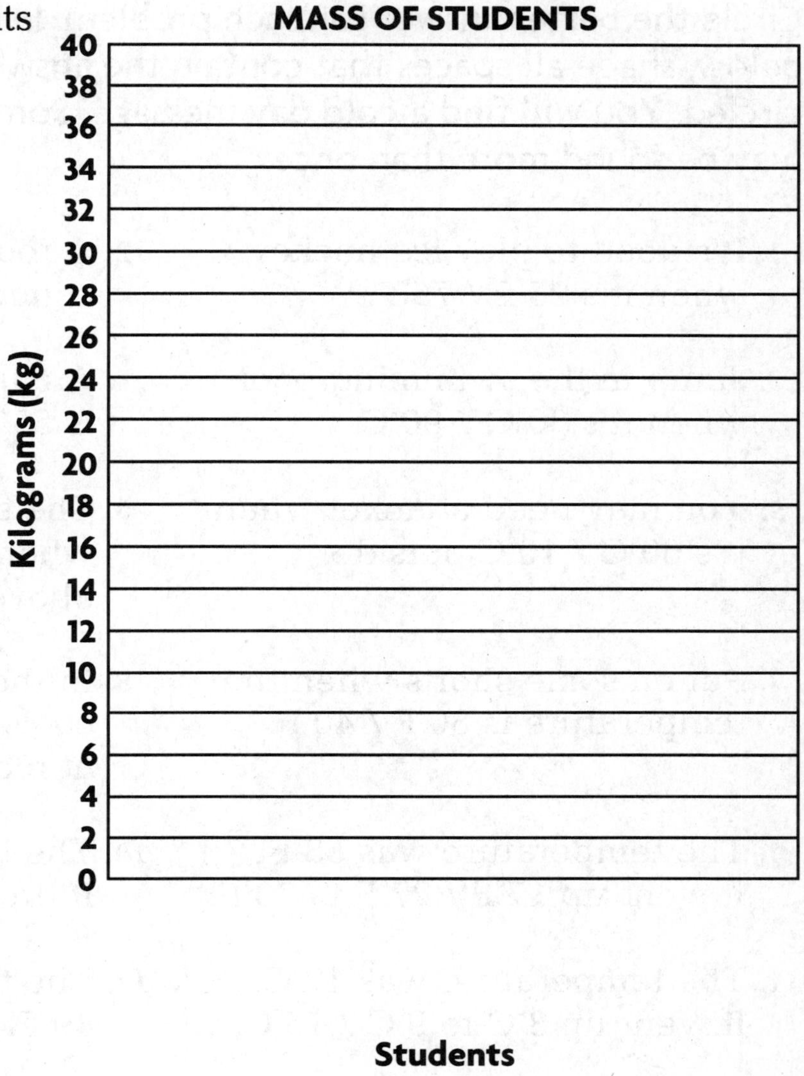

Student	Mass
Alice	31 kg
Bob	38 kg
Donna	29 kg
Elia	35 kg
Juan	33 kg

MASS OF STUDENTS

Kilograms (kg)

40
38
36
34
32
30
28
26
24
22
20
18
16
14
12
10
8
6
4
2
0

Students

1. Use the table to make a bar graph.
   Check students' graphs.

2. What is the difference between the least and greatest mass shown in the graph? ___9 kg___

3. What is the combined mass of Alice and Elia? ___66 kg___

4. Order the students from least mass to greatest mass.

   Donna, Alice, Juan, Elia, Bob

_____

_____

Name _____

A Cold Message

Circle the better answer for each problem. In the box below, shade all spaces that contain the answer you circled. You will find a cold day message. Some answers may be found more than once.

1. It's good to play ice hockey when it's (25°F) / 75°F.

2. A room that is 70°C / (20°C) is comfortable.

3. Jump in the swimming pool when it's (30°C) / 90°C.

4. A cup of soup is warm when it is 55°F / (110°F).

5. You may need a jacket when it's 60°C / (10°C) outside.

6. The snow should start to melt when the temperature rises above (0°C) / 35°C.

7. Put on some shorts when the temperature is (80°F) / 40°F.

8. In the summer, it sometimes cools down to 15°F / (60°F) at night.

9. The temperature was 53°F. It went up (17°F) / 27°F to 70°F.

10. The temperature was 26°C. It dropped 44°C / (8°C) to 18°C.

11. The temperature was 12°C. It went up 3°C to 9°C / (15°C).

12. The temperature was (39°F) / 49°F. It went up 25°F to 64°F.

13. The temperature was 24°C. It dropped 8°C to (16°C) / 6°C.

14. The temperature was 44°F / (72°F). It dropped 14°F to 58°F.

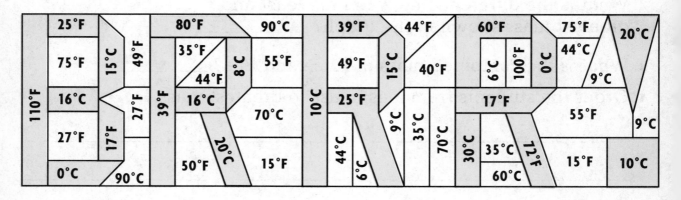

What's the Angle?

Play with a partner.

Materials:

- 12 index cards, ruler

How to Play:

- Draw angles on the back of each index card. Be sure to have 4 that are *right angles*, 4 that are *acute angles*, and 4 that are *obtuse angles*.

- Shuffle the cards and lay them, face down, in 3 rows with 4 cards in each row.

- The object is to win cards by matching angles.

- The first player turns 2 cards over. It they are both the same type of angle, the player wins the cards. If they are not the same type, turn them back over and the next player takes a turn.

- The player with the most cards at the end wins.

Examples:

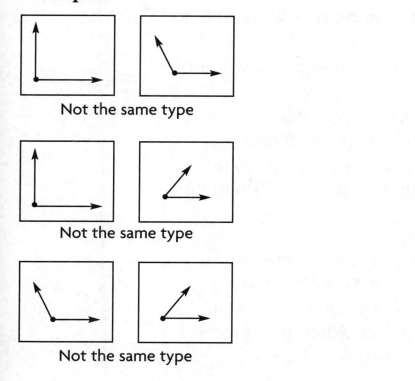

Not the same type

Not the same type

Not the same type

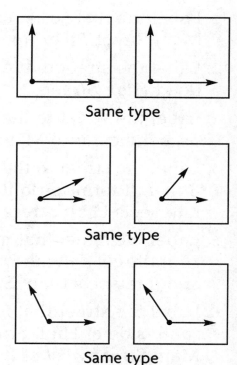

Same type

Same type

Same type

Mapmaker, Mapmaker, Make Me a Map!

Use the directions below and what you know about lines and angles to label the streets on the map.

Check students' answers.

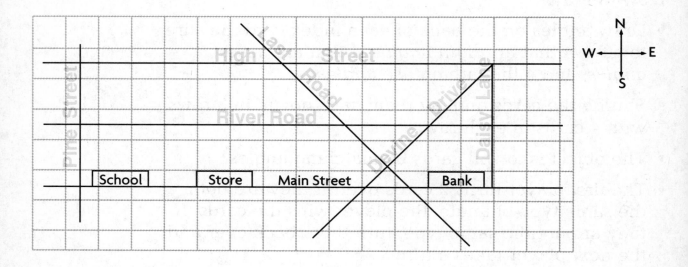

1. Label the first street to the north of and parallel to Main Street *River Road*.

2. Label the street to the north of and parallel to River Road *High Street*.

3. Label the street to the east of the bank and perpendicular to Main Street *Daisy Lane*.

4. Label the street to the west of the school *Pine Street*. It forms a right angle with Main Street and intersects High Street.

5. Label the street that meets Daisy Lane and High Street *Devine Drive*. It runs southwest and intersects Main Street east of the store.

6. Label the street that forms an obtuse angle on the south side of High Street *Last Road*. It intersects Main Street west of the bank.

Polygon Puzzle

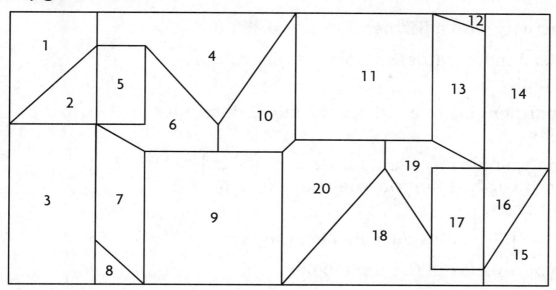

Answer the following questions and then follow the directions.

1. Write the numbers of the polygons that have 4 sides and 4 angles.

   1, 3, 5, 7, 9, 11, 13, 14, 15, 17

2. Write the numbers of the polygons that have 3 sides and 3 angles.

   2, 8, 12, 16

3. Write the numbers of the polygons that have 5 or more sides and 5 or more angles.

   4, 6, 10, 18, 19, 20

4. Use the chart to color the polygons.

5. Make your own design using polygons. Color the design. Check students' designs.

Numbers	Color
1, 15	Black
2, 16	Red
3, 14	Yellow
7, 13	Green
8, 12	Orange
5, 17	Purple
6, 19	Brown
10, 20	Blue
9, 11	Pink
4, 18	Light Blue

Name _____

Triangle Tally

Do this activity with a partner. Check students' work.

Materials: 3 index cards, scissors, pencil, ruler, sheet of paper

- Each partner cuts one index card into 3 different triangles.

- Sort the triangles by the number of equal sides. Use a ruler to verify if the triangles have 0, 2, or 3 equal sides.

- Trace the 6 triangles on a sheet of paper.

- Tally your results in the table below.

SIDES OF THE TRIANGLES

0 equal sides	2 equal sides	3 equal sides

- Sort the triangles by their angles. Use the corner of the third index card to see if each triangle has one right angle, one obtuse angle, or three acute angles.

- Tally your results in the table below.

ANGLES OF THE TRIANGLES

1 right angle	1 obtuse angle	3 acute angles

Quadrilateral Puzzles

Read the clues. Color the figures.
Write the name of each figure.

1. If a quadrilateral has 1 pair of parallel sides and 2 right angles, color it red.

2. If a quadrilateral has 4 right angles and 2 pairs of equal sides, color it blue.

3. If a quadrilateral has no equal sides and no right angles, color it green.

4. If a quadrilateral has 4 right angles and 4 equal sides, color it purple.

5. If a quadrilateral has one pair of parallel sides and no right angles, color it brown.

6. If a quadrilateral has 4 equal sides but has no right angles, color it orange.

7. If a quadrilateral has 6 right angles, color it black. There should be no quadrilaterals colored black.

8. If a quadrilateral has 2 pairs of parallel sides, no right angles, and 2 pairs of equal sides, color it pink.

9. If a quadrilateral has 1 right angle and 1 pair of parallel sides, color it gray. There should be no quadrilaterals colored gray.

10. If a quadrilateral has 4 right angles and no equal sides, color it yellow. There should be no quadrilaterals colored yellow.

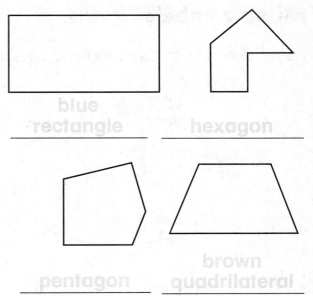

blue
rectangle _____   hexagon _____

pentagon _____   brown
quadrilateral _____

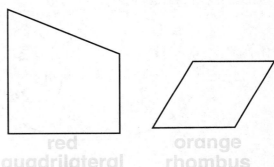

red
quadrilateral _____   orange
rhombus _____

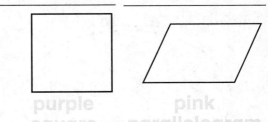

purple
square _____   pink
parallelogram _____

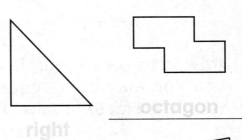

octagon _____

right
triangle _____

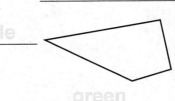

green
quadrilateral _____

Missing Labels

Label the sets in each Venn diagram below.

1. __Figures That Have__ __Figures That Have__
   __Straight Sides__ __Curved Sides__

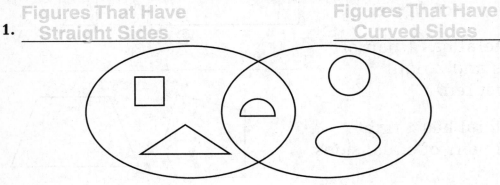

2. __Multiples of 3__ __Multiples of 4__

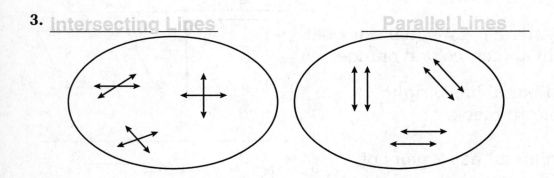

9
15
21
12
24
8
16
32

3. __Intersecting Lines__ __Parallel Lines__

4. Draw your own Venn diagram, but do not label the
   sets. You may use geometric figures or numbers.
   Ask a classmate to label the sets.
   Check students' diagrams.

Five Square

You can make several different shapes out of 5 congruent squares. At least 1 side of each square must touch the side of another square.

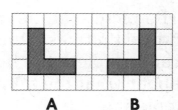

A   **B**

Look at the shapes. Shapes A and B are congruent. You can turn Shape A so it will fit on top of Shape B. Shapes C and D are not congruent.

C   **D**

Are the shapes congruent? Write *yes* or *no.*

1.
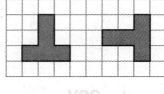
yes

2.
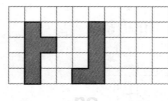
no

3.
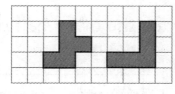
no

4.
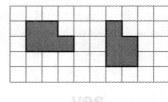
yes

5.
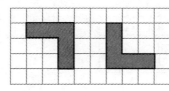
yes

6.
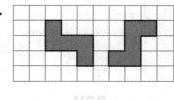
yes

You can make 12 different shapes with 5 congruent squares. At least 1 side of each square must touch the side of another square. The first 6 are done for you. Draw six more.

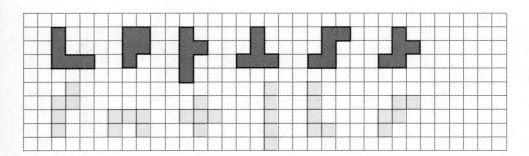

Symmetry

The picture at the right shows half of a figure that has a line of symmetry. You can complete the figure by thinking about what the mirror image would look like.

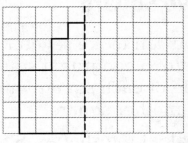

The second picture shows what the whole figure looks like.

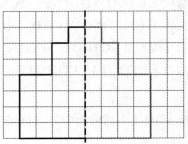

Draw the other half of the figure.

1.

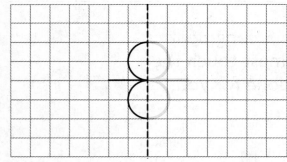

2.

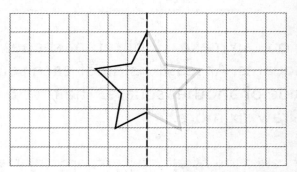

3.

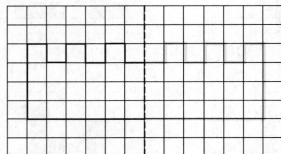

4.

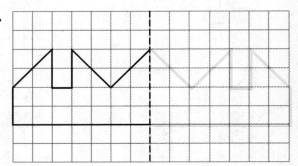

5.

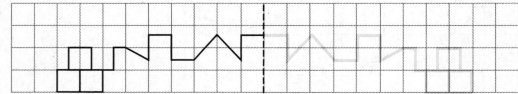

Measurement

You can make a small drawing larger. Look at the design on Grid 1. The columns and rows have numbers and letters. Now look at the larger grid. It has the same numbers and letters. Put your finger on the letter B on the small grid. Move your finger down the column until you reach the number 5. Find the B-5 square on the large grid. Draw the same part of the design from the small grid onto the large grid.

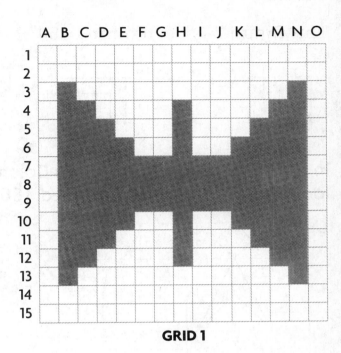

GRID 1

Shade in the same design on the larger grid. Use the numbers and letters to help you.

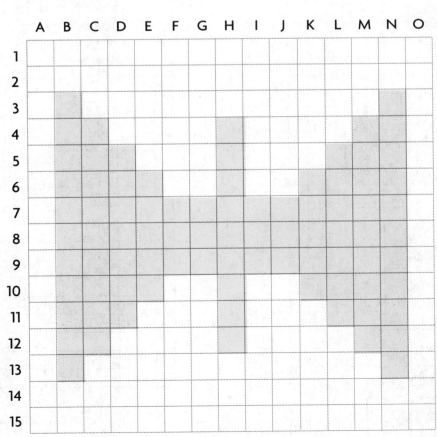

Turns

This figure has been turned 180°.

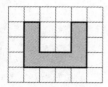)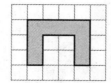

In Column B draw the figures in Column A as they would look after they have been turned 180°.

1.
2.
3.
4.
5.

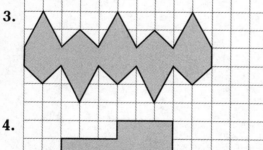

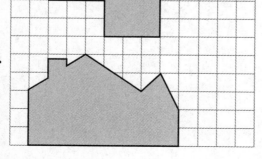

Tangrams

Tangrams are ancient Chinese puzzles. A square is divided into 7 pieces as shown below. Some or all of the pieces can be combined to make different shapes.

Trace the tangram puzzle. Then carefully cut apart the tangram pieces.

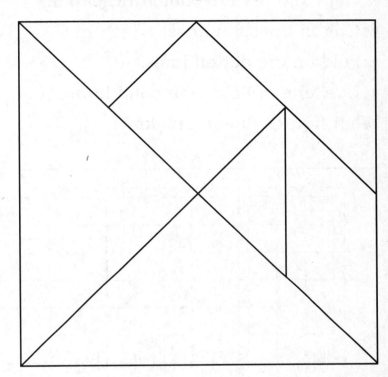

1. Use 2 pieces to make a square.

2. Use 3 pieces to make a parallelogram.

3. Use 6 pieces to make this fish.

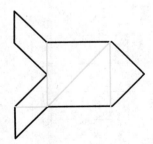

4. Try to put all 7 pieces back together again to make a square.

5. Make a shape with some or all of the tangram pieces. Draw the outline of the shape. Trade your outline for another student's and make the new shape.

Folding Solid Figures

You can make solid figures with paper. Look at the
patterns on this page.

- Copy the patterns onto grid paper.
- Cut on the solid lines.
- Fold on the dotted lines.
- Use tape to hold your solid figure together.

What figures did you make?

a rectangular prism and a cube

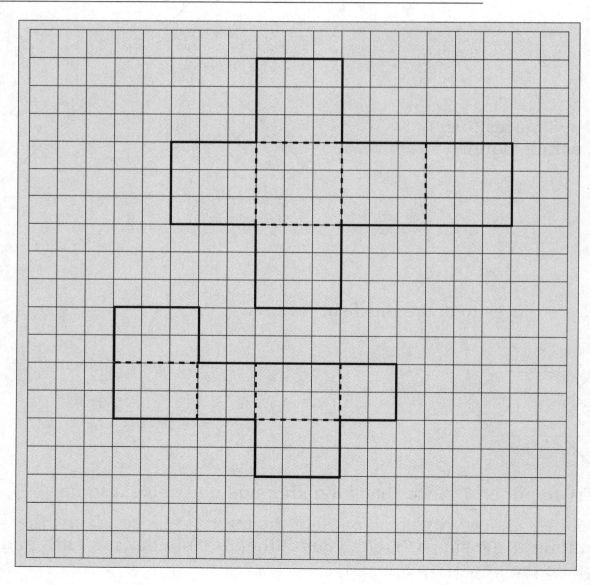

The Missing Half

Each figure below was once a cube, rectangular prism, square pyramid, sphere, cone, or cylinder. Each has been cut in half with one of the halves removed.

- Complete the solid figure.
- Name the solid figure. Check students' drawings.

1.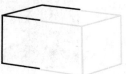

rectangular prism

2.

sphere

3.

square pyramid

4.

cylinder

5.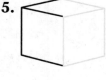

cube

6.

cone

Each figure below is made from two solids. One solid has been cut in half with one of the halves removed. Check students' drawings.

- Complete the figure. Name the solid figures.

7.

square pyramid; cube

8.

cone, cylinder

Tessellations

Use squares to make interesting tessellating shapes.

Materials: cardboard, scissors, tape, pencil, ruler, crayons

Directions:

Step 1: Cut a 2-inch by 2-inch square out of cardboard.

Step 2: Cut out a plane figure from one side of the square.

Step 3: Attach the cut-out plane figure to the opposite side of the square with tape.

Step 4: Put your new plane figure in the middle of the space below and trace it. Color the shape.

Step 5: Tessellate the figure until the space is covered.

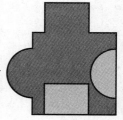

Try tessellating a figure with two shapes cut from the square.

Nets

Materials: ruler, scissors, tape

The figure at the right is called a **net**. It shows all the faces of a square pyramid. If you cut it out and folded it along the dotted lines, you can tape it together to make a square pyramid. On the dot paper below, draw a net for a cube or for a rectangular prism.

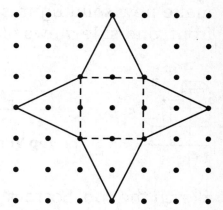

Check your work. Trace your net. Then cut it out and fold it. Tape the edges together. Does it make a cube or a rectangular prism? Check students' nets.

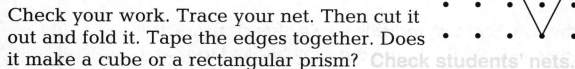

Different Views

You can put cubes together in many different ways to make new solid figures. When you do this, the top, front, and side views of the new figure may be different.

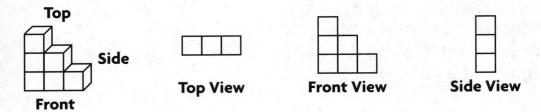

Top
Side
Front

Top View   Front View   Side View

Sketch the top, bottom, and side views of each figure. If you need help, build the figure out of cubes and look at it from different views.

	Top View	Front View	Side View
1.			
2.			
3.			
4.			

Find the Perimeter

Estimate the perimeter of each figure in centimeters (cm).
Then use a centimeter ruler to find the actual perimeter.

⊢━━⊣
1 cm

Estimates will vary.

1.

2 cm

estimate: _____ cm

perimeter: __8__ cm

2.

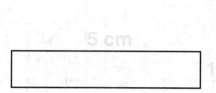

5 cm

1 cm

estimate: _____ cm

perimeter: __12__ cm

3.

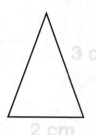

3 cm

2 cm

estimate: _____ cm

perimeter: __8__ cm

4.

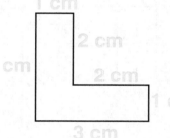

1 cm
2 cm
3 cm
2 cm
1 cm
3 cm

estimate: _____ cm

perimeter: __12__ cm

5.

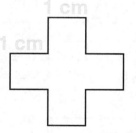

1 cm
1 cm

estimate: _____ cm

perimeter: __12__ cm

6.

2 cm
3 cm
3 cm

estimate: _____ cm

perimeter: __13__ cm

7.

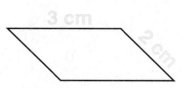

3 cm
2 cm

estimate: _____ cm

perimeter: __10__ cm

8.

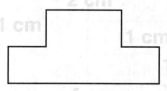

2 cm
1 cm
1 cm
1 cm
4 cm

estimate: _____ cm

perimeter: __12__ cm

9.

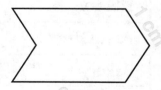

1 cm
3 cm

estimate: _____ cm

perimeter: __10__ cm

Areas in Town

Find the area of each building in the town drawn on the grid below. Record your findings in the table.

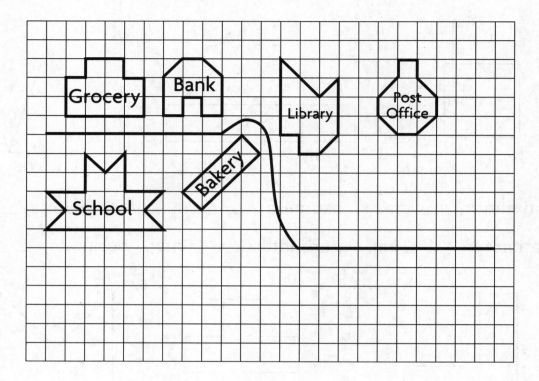

	Building	Area	
1.	Grocery	_10_	square units
2.	Bank	_7_	square units
3.	School	_13_	square units
4.	Library	_10_	square units
5.	Post Office	_8_	square units
6.	Bakery	_6_	square units

7. Add a toy shop to the town. Make it have an area of 9 square units. Drawings will vary. Check students' drawings.

8. Add a restaurant to the town. Make it have the same area as the toy shop but a different shape. Drawings will vary. Check students' drawings.

Painting Project

Amanda and her father are painting the walls of a playroom. One of the walls has a window. Another wall has a door, which they are not painting.

Find the area that needs to be painted on each of the four walls. All measurements are given in feet.

1.

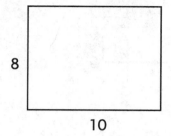

area = __80__ square feet

2.

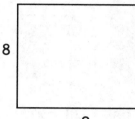

area = __72__ square feet

3.

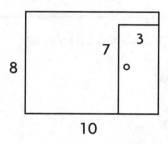

area = __59__ square feet

4.

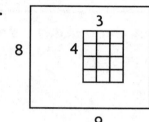

area = __60__ square feet

5. What is the total area that needs to be painted?

_____271 sq ft_____

6. The label on the can of paint says that 1 quart covers about 100 square feet. How many quarts of paint will Amanda and her father need to paint the walls with 2 coats of paint?

_____6 qt_____

7. Amanda wants to put a wallpaper border around the room near the ceiling. How many feet of wallpaper border does she need to go all the way around the room?

_____38 ft_____

Combining Volumes

Some solids are made by combining two or more
rectangular prisms. To find the volume of these
solids, first find the volume of each prism. Then
add the volumes.

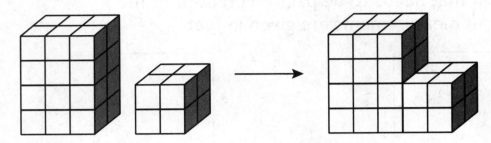

4 layers × 6 cubes = 24 cubic units

24 + 8 = 32 cubic units

2 layers × 4 cubes = 8 cubic units

Find the volume of each solid. Write the volume in cubic units.

1.

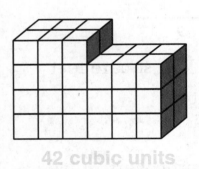

42 cubic units

2.

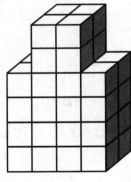

40 cubic units

3.

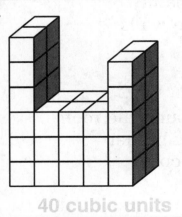

40 cubic units

4.

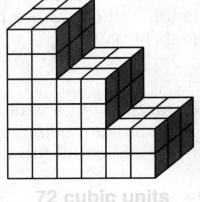

72 cubic units

Continue the Pattern

Find the pattern unit on each grid. Use it to continue
each pattern.

1.

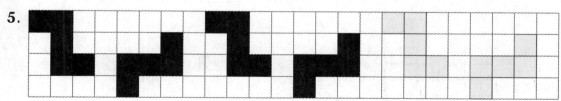

2.

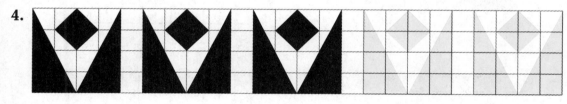

3.

4.

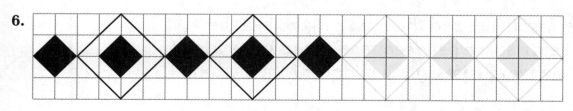

5.

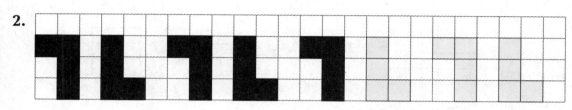

6.

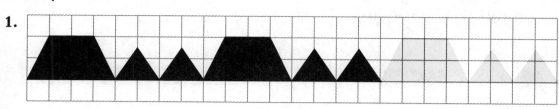

7. Use the grid to make your own pattern. Check students' work.

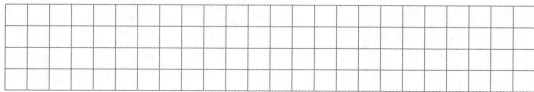

Missing Tiles

Two figures are missing from the middle of each tile pattern in the left column. Draw a line from each pattern in the left column to the missing figures in the right column.

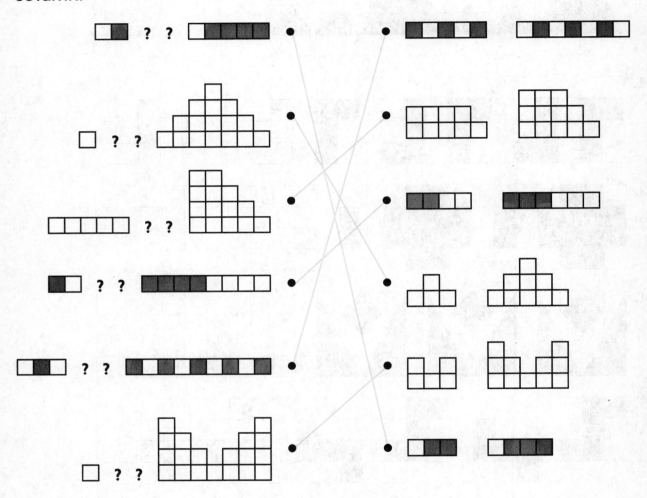

Draw the first figure and the fourth figure in a tile pattern. Leave space between the figures. Ask a friend to draw the two figures in the middle of the pattern.

Traveling Birds

Riddle: Why do birds fly south?

Find the missing numbers in the number patterns.

1. 93, 87, 81, 75, __69__, 63, __57__, __51__
              T   A   S

2. 30, 37, 44, 51, __58__, __65__, 72, __79__
             E   O   H

3. 245, 257, 269, 281, __293__, 305, __317__, __329__
            Y   A   L

4. 635, 626, 617, 608, __599__, __590__, 581, __572__
            T   K   T

5. 680, 655, 630, 605, __580__, __555__, 530, __505__
            B   E   K

6. 1,326; 1,426; 1,526; __1,626__; 1,726; __1,826__; __1,926__
            N   U   I

7. 2,036; 2,016; 1,996; 1,976; __1,956__; __1,936__; 1,916; __1,896__; __1,876__
            O   T   D   E

Now solve the riddle. Match each letter to the numbers you found in the number patterns. Write the letters on the lines below.

T H E Y   D O N ' T
599 79 555 293   1,896 65 1,626 572

L I K E   T O
329 1,926 590 1,876   69 1,956

T A K E   A   B U S
1,936 57 505 58   317   580 1,826 51

Number Pattern Game

95

124

276

301

87

365

159

283

Play with a partner.

Materials: Number cards shown at the left
Number cube with numbers 1–6
Paper and pencil

How to Play: Players take turns making number patterns.

Step 1 Cut out the number cards. Place them facedown on the table.

Step 2 Choose a number card for the starting number of a number pattern.

Step 3 Roll the number cube to find the number the player will add or subtract to make a number pattern. Decide the operation.

Step 4 Use the starting number and the rule to write the first five numbers in the pattern.

Step 5 At the end of the turn, write down the ones digit of the fifth number in the pattern.

Take turns repeating steps 1–5.

The game ends when all the number cards have been used. At the end of the game, add the digit from each turn. The player with more points at the end of the game wins.

Variation: Use two number cubes to form a 2-digit number to add or subtract to make a pattern.

Missing Numbers

Complete the patterns below. Then find the answers in the number search. Circle the answers. The numbers can be found going up, across, down, backward, and diagonally.

1. 225, 255, 285, __315__, 345, __375__, __405__

2. 5,423; 5,413; 5,403; __5,393__; __5,383__; 5,373; __5,363__

3. 764, __744__, __724__, 704, 684, 664, __644__

4. 3,240; __3,255__; __3,270__; __3,285__; 3,300; 3,315; 3,330

5. 160, 184, 208, __232__, __256__, 280, __304__

6. 948, __916__, __884__, __852__, 820, 788, 756

7. 3,460; 3,435; 3,410; __3,385__; 3,360; __3,335__; __3,310__

8. 2,154; 2,187; 2,220; __2,253__; __2,286__; 2,319; __2,352__

3	2	5	3	6	3	6	5	1	3
7	2	6	0	9	1	4	3	2	3
4	8	7	1	9	3	2	2	1	3
4	6	9	0	8	5	7	7	3	5
0	0	1	3	3	3	8	5	4	2
8	9	5	2	0	2	1	3	6	7
0	4	2	5	6	8	2	9	1	5
1	7	9	2	6	5	5	3	5	3
3	7	5	4	0	3	8	2	0	4
3	1	4	8	8	4	3	5	2	2

Dart Board Probability

A single dart can land anywhere on this dart board.
Tell whether each event is *certain*, *impossible*, *likely*,
or *unlikely*.

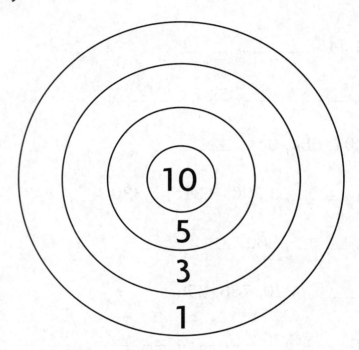

1. The score is an odd number. _____likely_____

2. The score is more than 3. _____unlikely_____

3. The score is 8. _____impossible_____

4. The score is 1 or 3. _____likely_____

5. The score is less than 10. _____likely_____

6. The score is the product of 3 × 5. _____impossible_____

7. The dart lands on the number 3. _____unlikely_____

8. The score is less than 12. _____certain_____

9. The score is greater than 1. _____likely_____

10. The score is 5. _____unlikely_____

11. The score is 10. _____unlikely_____

12. The score is an odd or even number. _____certain_____

Design It!

Work with a partner.

Materials: crayons, paper clip, pencil

Step 1: Use the blank spinner at the right. Use the guide lines to design a spinner that will enable you to spin red 60 out of 100 times. Use as many or as few colors as you like. In the table, list the colors that you use.

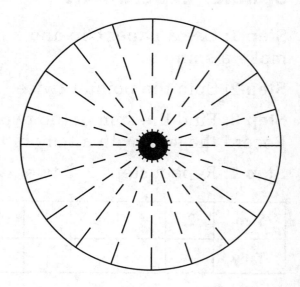

Step 2: Use a paper clip and pencil to make a spinner. Test your spinner by conducting 100 spins and recording the results in the table below.

Check students' work. Answers will vary.

Color	Results of Spins
Red	

1. What are the possible outcomes on your spinner?

   _____

2. What are the chances of spinning a red on your spinner?

   _____

3. How do the chances of spinning a red on your spinner compare with the desired chances of 60 out of 100?

   _____

4. After using your spinner 100 times, would you change your spinner in any way? If so, how would you change it and why?

   _____

Spinner Experiment

Step 1: Use a paper clip and a pencil to make a spinner.

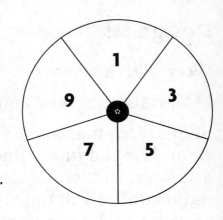

Step 2: Spin the pointer twice.

Step 3: Find the sum of the two numbers. Record the sum with a tally in the table below.

Step 4: Repeat steps 2–3 twenty-five times.

Check students' work.

Sum	2	4	6	8	10	12	14	16	18
Tally									

1. What are the possible outcomes?

   Sums of 2, 4, 6, 8, 10, 12, 14, 16, and 18

2. Which sum did you spin most often?

   Answers will vary.

3. Is the chance of spinning a sum that is an odd number certain, likely, unlikely, or impossible?

   impossible

4. If you were to use the spinner one more time, what would you predict the sum would be?

   Answers will vary.

5. Which would you predict is more likely to occur: spinning a sum that is less than 10 or a sum that is equal to or greater than 10?

   Answers will vary. There are more outcomes with sums 10 or greater.

6. Which would you predict is more likely to occur, a sum of 10 or a sum of 2? Explain.

   Sum of 10; There are 5 outcomes with a sum of 10 and only 1 outcome with a sum of 2.

Name _____

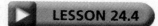

Nature Hunt

Mrs. Brown's third-grade class is going on a nature hunt. The class is arranged in four groups. Each group has been given a list of items to find. They have ten minutes to find what is on the list. Look at the pictures, and then answer the following questions. The items pictured are the ones on the list.

1. Is it likely or unlikely that one group won't find any of the items?

Possible answers: unlikely

because all the items seem

fairly common.

_____

2. If one group has only two people, what is the most likely outcome of their hunt?

Possible answer: They may

not find everything in

ten minutes.

_____

3. Mrs. Brown told the four groups each to make up a name that relates to nature. What are some possible names for groups?

Answers will vary: any name

that has to do with nature

4. If Mrs. Brown teaches in Minnesota, in which season is she least likely to take her class out on a nature hunt?

winter

Combinations and Probability

You can make a tree diagram to show all the possible combinations if you tossed two coins at the same time.

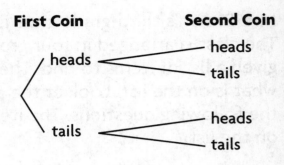

First Coin   **Second Coin**

1. Make a tree diagram to show all the possible combinations if you tossed a coin and rolled a cube numbered 1 through 6.

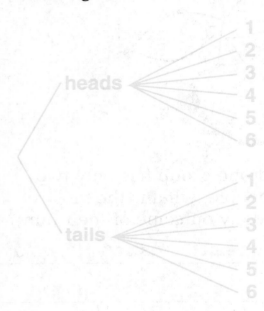

For 2-6, use your tree diagram to determine whether each combination is *impossible*, *unlikely*, *likely*, or *certain*.

2. tails and 2 _____unlikely_____

3. tails and an odd number _____unlikely_____

4. heads or tails and a number less than 7 _____certain_____

5. heads and tails _____impossible_____

6. heads or tails and a number greater than 1 _____likely_____

7. Use your tree diagram. Name two combinations that are equally likely.

   _____Possible answer: heads and a number less than 7;_____

   _____tails and a number less than 7_____

A Trip to the Science Museum

Vernon went to the science museum with his mother, father, and sister. Make a list to solve each problem about Vernon's trip to the museum. Use the back of your paper if you need more space.

1. Vernon visited a model of the heart, the rainforest, and the mummy exhibit. In how many different orders could he have visited these areas?

heart, rainforest, mummy
heart, mummy, rainforest
rainforest, heart, mummy
rainforest, mummy, heart
mummy, heart, rainforest
mummy, rainforest, heart

_____ 6 ways _____

2. Vernon's sister bought posters of a koala, a tornado, and a dolphin. In how many different ways will she be able to hang these posters in a row on her bedroom wall?

koala, tornado, dolphin
koala, dolphin, tornado
tornado, koala, dolphin
tornado, dolphin, koala
dolphin, koala, tornado
dolphin, tornado, koala

_____ 6 ways _____

3. Only one person at a time can go through the turnstile at the entrance to the museum. In how many different ways could Vernon and his family have entered the museum?

Vernon, mother, father, sister
Vernon, mother, sister, father
Vernon, father, mother, sister
Vernon, father, sister, mother
Vernon, sister, mother, father
Vernon, sister, father, mother
mother, Vernon, father, sister
mother, Vernon, sister, father
mother, father, Vernon, sister
mother, father, sister, Vernon
mother, sister, Vernon, father
mother sister, father, Vernon
father, Vernon, mother, sister
father, Vernon, sister, mother
father, mother, Vernon, sister
father, mother, sister, Vernon
father, sister, Vernon, mother
father, sister, mother, Vernon
sister, Vernon, mother, father
sister, Vernon, father, mother
sister, mother, Vernon, father
sister, mother, father, Vernon
sister, father, Vernon, mother
sister, father, mother, Vernon

_____ 24 ways _____

Name _____

Fetching Fractions

Find the word name in Column 2 for each fraction in
Column 1. Then write the word name's circled letter on
the line in front of the fraction.

Column 1		Column 2	
_L_	1. $\frac{1}{2}$	(A)	two fifths
_S_	2. $\frac{3}{4}$	(C)	two ninths
_A_	3. $\frac{2}{5}$	(E)	five divided by nine
_W_	4. $\frac{1}{3}$	(F)	one out of four
_O_	5. $\frac{6}{10}$	(H)	one tenth
_C_	6. $\frac{2}{9}$	(I)	seven divided by eight
_F_	7. $\frac{1}{4}$	(L)	one out of two
_E_	8. $\frac{5}{9}$	(N)	four eighths
_N_	9. $\frac{4}{8}$	(O)	six tenths
_H_	10. $\frac{1}{10}$	(P)	one out of five
_T_	11. $\frac{5}{6}$	(R)	eight ninths
_P_	12. $\frac{1}{5}$	(S)	three divided by four
_I_	13. $\frac{7}{8}$	(T)	five sixths
_R_	14. $\frac{8}{9}$	(W)	one out of three

Now decode the sentence below. The numbers tell you where to look
in Column 1. Write the letter that is on the blank in front of the number.

$\frac{A}{3}$ $\frac{F}{7}$ $\frac{R}{14}$ $\frac{A}{3}$ $\frac{C}{6}$ $\frac{T}{11}$ $\frac{I}{13}$ $\frac{O}{5}$ $\frac{N}{9}$ $\frac{I}{13}$ $\frac{S}{2}$.

$\frac{P}{12}$ $\frac{A}{3}$ $\frac{R}{14}$ $\frac{T}{11}$ $\frac{O}{5}$ $\frac{F}{7}$ $\frac{A}{3}$ $\frac{W}{4}$ $\frac{H}{10}$ $\frac{O}{5}$ $\frac{L}{1}$ $\frac{E}{8}$.

CW130 Challenge

Color the Apples

How could you color $\frac{3}{4}$ of 8 apples red?

Look at the *denominator*.

It tells you to make
4 equal parts.

Divide the 8 apples into
4 equal groups.

Each group has 2 apples.

Look at the *numerator*.

It tells you to color
3 of the groups.

Color 3 of the 4 groups.

The picture shows 3 groups
or 6 apples shaded.

So, $\frac{3}{4}$ of 8 = 6.

Color the apples to show the part of the group the
fraction names. Solve. Check students' coloring.

1.

Color $\frac{1}{4}$ red.

$\frac{1}{4}$ of 12 = ___3___

2.

Color $\frac{3}{4}$ green.

$\frac{3}{4}$ of 12 = ___9___

3.

Color $\frac{1}{5}$ green.

$\frac{1}{5}$ of 15 = ___3___

4.

Color $\frac{2}{5}$ red.

$\frac{2}{5}$ of 15 = ___6___

Challenge   CW131

Criss-Cross-Match

You can always use criss-cross-match to see if fractions are equivalent. How does it work? First, multiply the numerator of the first fraction by the denominator of the second and write the product down. Then, multiply the numerator of the second fraction by the denominator of the first and write that product down. If the products match, the fractions are equivalent.

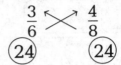

These fractions are equivalent.

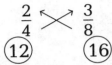

These fractions are not equivalent.

Use criss-cross-match to find the fractions that are equivalent to the fraction in the center box. Shade the fractions that are equivalent.

1.

$\frac{9}{9}$	$\frac{4}{20}$	$\frac{6}{25}$
$\frac{5}{10}$	$\frac{1}{5}$	$\frac{3}{8}$
$\frac{7}{35}$	$\frac{5}{6}$	$\frac{2}{10}$

2.

$\frac{2}{2}$	$\frac{9}{13}$	$\frac{15}{15}$
$\frac{8}{11}$	$\frac{8}{8}$	$\frac{10}{11}$
$\frac{9}{9}$	$\frac{5}{10}$	$\frac{3}{4}$

3.

$\frac{4}{5}$	$\frac{5}{10}$	$\frac{2}{7}$
$\frac{8}{11}$	$\frac{1}{2}$	$\frac{4}{8}$
$\frac{3}{6}$	$\frac{4}{5}$	$\frac{2}{3}$

4.

$\frac{7}{13}$	$\frac{9}{12}$	$\frac{2}{9}$
$\frac{2}{7}$	$\frac{3}{4}$	$\frac{5}{11}$
$\frac{12}{16}$	$\frac{6}{8}$	$\frac{4}{13}$

5.

$\frac{9}{27}$	$\frac{4}{40}$	$\frac{3}{18}$
$\frac{2}{12}$	$\frac{1}{6}$	$\frac{7}{35}$
$\frac{5}{20}$	$\frac{11}{28}$	$\frac{4}{24}$

6.

$\frac{6}{9}$	$\frac{4}{5}$	$\frac{7}{8}$
$\frac{5}{6}$	$\frac{2}{3}$	$\frac{1}{2}$
$\frac{8}{12}$	$\frac{9}{13}$	$\frac{4}{6}$

Comparing Fractions

You can also use criss-cross-match to compare fractions.
How does it work? Look at these examples.

$\frac{3}{4} \diagup\!\!\!\!\diagdown \frac{2}{5}$

$5 \times 3 = 15 \quad 4 \times 2 = 8$

$15 > 8$

So, $\frac{3}{4} > \frac{2}{5}$.

$\frac{4}{9} \diagup\!\!\!\!\diagdown \frac{5}{8}$

$8 \times 4 = 32 \quad 9 \times 5 = 45$

$32 < 45$

So, $\frac{4}{9} < \frac{5}{8}$.

Use criss-cross-match to compare the fractions to the
fraction in the center box. Shade the fractions that are
greater than the fraction in the center box.

1.

$\frac{2}{3}$	$\frac{3}{5}$	$\frac{2}{7}$
$\frac{4}{10}$	$\frac{1}{2}$	$\frac{1}{4}$
$\frac{3}{8}$	$\frac{2}{6}$	$\frac{7}{8}$

2.

$\frac{4}{8}$	$\frac{5}{6}$	$\frac{2}{2}$
$\frac{6}{7}$	$\frac{2}{3}$	$\frac{1}{2}$
$\frac{3}{4}$	$\frac{4}{5}$	$\frac{10}{10}$

3.

$\frac{1}{2}$	$\frac{2}{3}$	$\frac{7}{8}$
$\frac{4}{6}$	$\frac{5}{6}$	$\frac{9}{10}$
$\frac{3}{5}$	$\frac{4}{5}$	$\frac{6}{7}$

4.

$\frac{2}{5}$	$\frac{1}{2}$	$\frac{1}{3}$
$\frac{6}{9}$	$\frac{3}{7}$	$\frac{4}{4}$
$\frac{6}{8}$	$\frac{4}{10}$	$\frac{4}{6}$

5.

$\frac{1}{9}$	$\frac{1}{8}$	$\frac{1}{7}$
$\frac{1}{5}$	$\frac{1}{6}$	$\frac{1}{1}$
$\frac{1}{4}$	$\frac{1}{3}$	$\frac{1}{2}$

6.

$\frac{2}{3}$	$\frac{7}{8}$	$\frac{2}{4}$
$\frac{5}{7}$	$\frac{10}{10}$	$\frac{7}{9}$
$\frac{8}{9}$	$\frac{3}{4}$	$\frac{5}{6}$

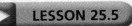
Name _____

Fraction Patterns

Look at the bottom of the page for the missing fraction in each fraction pattern below. Write on the line above the missing fraction the circled letter that is next to the fraction pattern. (Some letters appear more than once.)

1. $\dfrac{5}{16}$, $\dfrac{4}{16}$, $\underline{\dfrac{3}{16}}$, $\dfrac{2}{16}$ Ⓡ

2. $\dfrac{1}{9}$, $\dfrac{2}{9}$, $\underline{\dfrac{3}{9}}$, $\dfrac{4}{9}$ Ⓝ

3. $\dfrac{2}{10}$, $\dfrac{4}{10}$, $\dfrac{6}{10}$, $\underline{\dfrac{8}{10}}$ Ⓣ

4. $\dfrac{9}{12}$, $\underline{\dfrac{10}{12}}$, $\dfrac{11}{12}$, $\dfrac{12}{12}$ Ⓔ

5. $\dfrac{1}{12}$, $\dfrac{3}{12}$, $\dfrac{5}{12}$, $\underline{\dfrac{7}{12}}$ Ⓢ

6. $\dfrac{2}{8}$, $\dfrac{4}{8}$, $\underline{\dfrac{6}{8}}$, $\dfrac{8}{8}$ Ⓕ

7. $\dfrac{4}{20}$, $\dfrac{8}{20}$, $\dfrac{12}{20}$, $\underline{\dfrac{16}{20}}$ Ⓐ

8. $\dfrac{3}{16}$, $\dfrac{6}{16}$, $\dfrac{9}{16}$, $\underline{\dfrac{12}{16}}$ Ⓛ

9. $\dfrac{1}{6}$, $\underline{\dfrac{2}{6}}$, $\dfrac{3}{6}$, $\dfrac{4}{6}$ Ⓞ

10. $\dfrac{3}{15}$, $\dfrac{6}{15}$, $\dfrac{9}{15}$, $\underline{\dfrac{12}{15}}$ Ⓥ

11. $\dfrac{2}{18}$, $\dfrac{4}{18}$, $\dfrac{6}{18}$, $\underline{\dfrac{8}{18}}$ Ⓘ

12. $\dfrac{5}{30}$, $\dfrac{10}{30}$, $\dfrac{15}{30}$, $\underline{\dfrac{20}{30}}$ Ⓗ

13. $\dfrac{4}{24}$, $\dfrac{7}{24}$, $\dfrac{10}{24}$, $\underline{\dfrac{13}{24}}$ Ⓒ

F R A C T I O N S

$\dfrac{6}{8}$ $\dfrac{3}{16}$ $\dfrac{16}{20}$ $\dfrac{13}{24}$ $\dfrac{8}{10}$ $\dfrac{8}{18}$ $\dfrac{2}{6}$ $\dfrac{3}{9}$ $\dfrac{7}{12}$

L O V E T O S H A R E.

$\dfrac{12}{16}$ $\dfrac{2}{6}$ $\dfrac{12}{15}$ $\dfrac{10}{12}$ $\dfrac{8}{10}$ $\dfrac{2}{6}$ $\dfrac{7}{12}$ $\dfrac{20}{30}$ $\dfrac{16}{20}$ $\dfrac{3}{16}$ $\dfrac{10}{12}$

Figure It Out

Look at Figure A. Suppose it equals $\frac{1}{2}$. What mixed number does Figure B equal?

Figure A

Figure B has 3 parts that are the same as Figure A. It shows $\frac{3}{2}$. The mixed number for $\frac{3}{2}$ is $1\frac{1}{2}$.

So, Figure B equals $1\frac{1}{2}$.

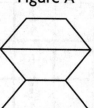

Figure B

Solve.

1. Figure C equals $\frac{1}{2}$. What mixed number does Figure D equal?

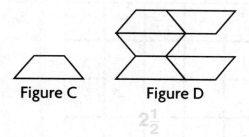

Figure C   Figure D

$2\frac{1}{2}$

2. Figure E equals $\frac{1}{4}$. What mixed number does Figure F equal?

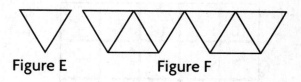

Figure E   Figure F

$1\frac{2}{4}$ or $1\frac{1}{2}$

3. Figure G equals $\frac{1}{5}$. What mixed number does Figure H equal?

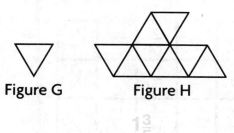

Figure G   Figure H

$1\frac{3}{5}$

4. Figure J equals $\frac{2}{3}$. What mixed number does Figure K equal?

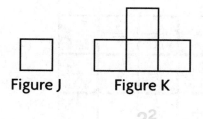

Figure J   Figure K

$2\frac{2}{3}$

5. Draw a figure by using parts that are the same size as Figure G. Make your figure equal $2\frac{1}{5}$.

Students' drawings should show 11 triangles.

Name _____

Fraction Squares

Fill in the empty squares to have correct addition across and down.

1.

$\frac{1}{4}$	+	$\frac{1}{4}$	=	$\frac{2}{4}$
+		+		+
$\frac{1}{4}$	+	$\frac{1}{4}$	=	$\frac{2}{4}$
=		=		=
$\frac{2}{4}$	+	$\frac{2}{4}$	=	$\frac{4}{4}$

2.

$\frac{1}{6}$	+	$\frac{2}{6}$	=	$\frac{3}{6}$
+		+		+
$\frac{1}{6}$	+	$\frac{1}{6}$	=	$\frac{2}{6}$
=		=		=
$\frac{2}{6}$	+	$\frac{3}{6}$	=	$\frac{5}{6}$

3.

$\frac{2}{10}$	+	$\frac{4}{10}$	=	$\frac{6}{10}$
+		+		+
$\frac{2}{10}$	+	$\frac{1}{10}$	=	$\frac{3}{10}$
=		=		=
$\frac{4}{10}$	+	$\frac{5}{10}$	=	$\frac{9}{10}$

4.

$\frac{4}{12}$	+	$\frac{3}{12}$	=	$\frac{7}{12}$
+		+		+
$\frac{3}{12}$	+	$\frac{1}{12}$	=	$\frac{4}{12}$
=		=		=
$\frac{7}{12}$	+	$\frac{4}{12}$	=	$\frac{11}{12}$

5.

$\frac{6}{20}$	+	$\frac{5}{20}$	=	$\frac{11}{20}$
+		+		+
$\frac{4}{20}$	+	$\frac{3}{20}$	=	$\frac{7}{20}$
=		=		=
$\frac{10}{20}$	+	$\frac{8}{20}$	=	$\frac{18}{20}$

6.

$\frac{2}{14}$	+	$\frac{5}{14}$	=	$\frac{7}{14}$
+		+		+
$\frac{3}{14}$	+	$\frac{2}{14}$	=	$\frac{5}{14}$
=		=		=
$\frac{5}{14}$	+	$\frac{7}{14}$	=	$\frac{12}{14}$

Fraction Puzzle

The fraction puzzle below has 21 pieces. The pieces are not all the same size. Trace the fraction bars. Be sure to make the number of each size of fraction bar that is shown to the left of the bars. Cut the bars out and label them with the correct fractions. Arrange the pieces on the fraction puzzle so that the 21 fraction bars fit on the puzzle. Glue the pieces to the puzzle. Possible arrangement given.

one:
$$1$$

one:
$$\frac{1}{2}$$

two:
$$\frac{1}{3}$$

two:
$$\frac{1}{4}$$

four:
$$\frac{1}{6}$$

five:
$$\frac{1}{5}$$

six:
$$\frac{1}{9}$$

		1		
$\frac{1}{4}$		$\frac{1}{4}$	$\frac{1}{6}$	$\frac{1}{3}$
$\frac{1}{9}$ $\frac{1}{9}$ $\frac{1}{9}$	$\frac{1}{6}$		$\frac{1}{2}$	
$\frac{1}{5}$	$\frac{1}{5}$	$\frac{1}{5}$	$\frac{1}{5}$	$\frac{1}{5}$
$\frac{1}{3}$	$\frac{1}{6}$	$\frac{1}{6}$	$\frac{1}{9}$	$\frac{1}{9}$ $\frac{1}{9}$

Find the Difference

Fill in the empty squares to have correct subtraction across and down.

1.

$\frac{6}{6}$	−	$\frac{3}{6}$	=	$\frac{3}{6}$
−		−		−
$\frac{4}{6}$	−	$\frac{2}{6}$	=	$\frac{2}{6}$
=		=		=
$\frac{2}{6}$	−	$\frac{1}{6}$	=	$\frac{1}{6}$

2.

$\frac{9}{10}$	−	$\frac{3}{10}$	=	$\frac{6}{10}$
−		−		−
$\frac{5}{10}$	−	$\frac{2}{10}$	=	$\frac{3}{10}$
=		=		=
$\frac{4}{10}$	−	$\frac{1}{10}$	=	$\frac{3}{10}$

3.

$\frac{9}{12}$	−	$\frac{4}{12}$	=	$\frac{5}{12}$
−		−		−
$\frac{6}{12}$	−	$\frac{2}{12}$	=	$\frac{4}{12}$
=		=		=
$\frac{3}{12}$	−	$\frac{2}{12}$	=	$\frac{1}{12}$

4.

$\frac{8}{9}$	−	$\frac{3}{9}$	=	$\frac{5}{9}$
−		−		−
$\frac{4}{9}$	−	$\frac{1}{9}$	=	$\frac{3}{9}$
=		=		=
$\frac{4}{9}$	−	$\frac{2}{9}$	=	$\frac{2}{9}$

5.

$\frac{18}{20}$	−	$\frac{10}{20}$	=	$\frac{8}{20}$
−		−		−
$\frac{9}{20}$	−	$\frac{2}{20}$	=	$\frac{7}{20}$
=		=		=
$\frac{9}{20}$	−	$\frac{8}{20}$	=	$\frac{1}{20}$

6.

$\frac{12}{14}$	−	$\frac{5}{14}$	=	$\frac{7}{14}$
−		−		−
$\frac{4}{14}$	−	$\frac{1}{14}$	=	$\frac{3}{14}$
=		=		=
$\frac{8}{14}$	−	$\frac{4}{14}$	=	$\frac{4}{14}$

Solve the Riddle

Look at the bottom of the page for the answer to each subtraction problem in simplest form. Write on the line above the answer the circled letter that is next to the subtraction problem. (Some letters appear more than once.)

1. $\frac{8}{10} - \frac{3}{10} =$ ____$\frac{1}{2}$____ (O)

2. $\frac{11}{12} - \frac{1}{12} =$ ____$\frac{5}{6}$____ (S)

3. $\frac{9}{12} - \frac{1}{12} =$ ____$\frac{2}{3}$____ (E)

4. $\frac{5}{8} - \frac{4}{8} =$ ____$\frac{1}{8}$____ (U)

5. $\frac{5}{6} - \frac{3}{6} =$ ____$\frac{1}{3}$____ (T)

6. $\frac{8}{12} - \frac{6}{12} =$ ____$\frac{1}{6}$____ (N)

7. $\frac{7}{8} - \frac{5}{8} =$ ____$\frac{1}{4}$____ (R)

8. $\frac{4}{5} - \frac{2}{5} =$ ____$\frac{2}{5}$____ (M)

9. $\frac{6}{10} - \frac{4}{10} =$ ____$\frac{1}{5}$____ (P)

10. $\frac{8}{8} - \frac{2}{8} =$ ____$\frac{3}{4}$____ (A)

N	U	M	E	R	A	T	O	R	S
$\frac{1}{6}$	$\frac{1}{8}$	$\frac{2}{5}$	$\frac{2}{3}$	$\frac{1}{4}$	$\frac{3}{4}$	$\frac{1}{3}$	$\frac{1}{2}$	$\frac{1}{4}$	$\frac{5}{6}$

A	R	E
$\frac{3}{4}$	$\frac{1}{4}$	$\frac{2}{3}$

T	O	P	S
$\frac{1}{3}$	$\frac{1}{2}$	$\frac{1}{5}$	$\frac{5}{6}$

Musical Math

These problems have all been solved by the Musical Mathematicians. Their answers are not all reasonable. Read the problems. Decide if the answers given are reasonable. If an answer is not reasonable, explain why.

Possible explanations are given.

1. A band played for a party. $\frac{4}{10}$ of the songs they played were Country Western, $\frac{3}{10}$ were Rock and Roll, and the rest were Jazz. What fraction of their songs were Jazz?

$\frac{3}{10}$ **were Jazz.**

The answer is reasonable.

2. During a break, some of the band members shared a pizza. The singer and the drummer each ate $\frac{3}{12}$ of the pizza. The rest of the pizza was saved until the next break. How much of the pizza was saved?

$\frac{1}{4}$ **was saved.** Since $\frac{3}{12} + \frac{3}{12} =$ $\frac{6}{12}$, or $\frac{1}{2}$, then $\frac{1}{2}$ of the pizza was eaten, so $\frac{1}{2}$ is still there.

The answer is not reasonable.

3. The guests at the party were asked if they liked the band's music. $\frac{5}{10}$ said they did and $\frac{4}{10}$ of the guests said they did not. The other guests could not decide. What part of the guests at the party could not decide?

$\frac{2}{5}$ **could not decide.**

Since $\frac{5}{10} + \frac{4}{10} = \frac{9}{10}$ and $\frac{10}{10} - \frac{9}{10} = \frac{1}{10}$, the answer is not reasonable.

4. The room where the party was held was divided into sections. The band used $\frac{1}{6}$ of the room. The food tables used $\frac{1}{6}$ of the room. The rest of the room was used by the guests. How much of the room was used by the guests?

$\frac{2}{3}$ **was used by the guests.**

The answer is reasonable.

Riddlegram!

Answer this riddle. Write the letter that matches each fraction or decimal. You will use some models more than once.

Riddle: Why do you measure snakes in inches?

B E C A U S E $\underset{0.2}{T}$ $\underset{\frac{7}{10}}{H}$ $\underset{\frac{5}{10}}{E}$ $\underset{0.9}{Y}$

$\underset{0.7}{H}$ $\underset{\frac{1}{10}}{A}$ $\underset{0.4}{V}$ $\underset{\frac{5}{10}}{E}$ $\underset{0.3}{N}$ $\underset{\frac{8}{10}}{O}$ $\underset{\frac{6}{10}}{F}$ $\underset{0.5}{E}$ $\underset{0.5}{E}$ $\underset{\frac{2}{10}}{T}$!

T
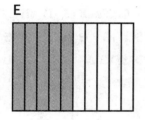

E
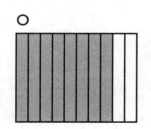

Y
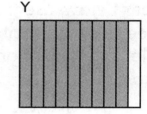

N
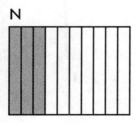

O
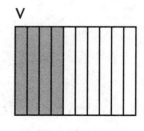

V
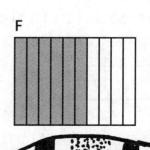

H
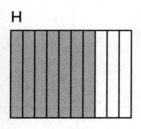

A
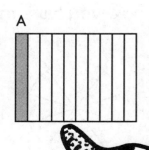

F

Add It Up

Each circle or bar is divided into tenths. Use two crayons in different colors to show two decimal numbers that equal one whole. Then complete the equation below the picture to show how you have made one whole. The first one has been done for you. Check students' drawings and equations.

1.

__0.3__ + __0.7__ = 1.0

2.
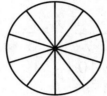

___ + ___ = 1.0

3.
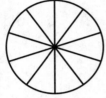

___ + ___ = 1.0

4.

___ + ___ = 1.0

5.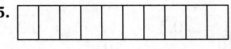

___ + ___ = 1.0

For each circle or bar below, use three crayons in different colors to show three decimal numbers that equal one whole. Then complete the equation to show how you have made one whole. Check students' drawings and equations.

6.

___ + ___ + ___ = 1.0

7.
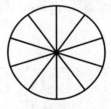

___ + ___ + ___ = 1.0

For each circle or bar below, use four crayons in different colors to show four decimal numbers that equal one whole. Then complete the equation to show how you have made one whole. Check students' drawings and equations.

8.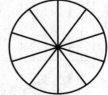

___ + ___ + ___ + ___ = 1.0

9.

___ + ___ + ___ + ___ = 1.0

Name _____

Pieces and Parts

Write a decimal to show what part of each decimal model
is shaded and a decimal to show what part is not shaded.

1.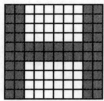

Shaded: ___0.52___

Not shaded: ___0.48___

2.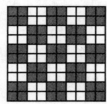

Shaded: ___0.52___

Not shaded: ___0.48___

3.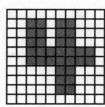

Shaded: ___0.32___

Not shaded: ___0.68___

4.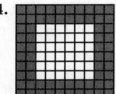

Shaded: ___0.64___

Not shaded: ___0.36___

5.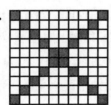

Shaded: ___0.20___

Not shaded: ___0.80___

6.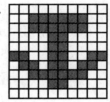

Shaded: ___0.36___

Not shaded: ___0.64___

Draw and shade a design for each decimal model.
Then write a decimal to show what part of each
decimal model is shaded and a decimal to show
what part is not shaded.

Check students' designs and answers. Answers will vary.

7.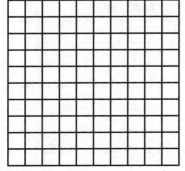

Shaded: _____

Not Shaded: _____

8.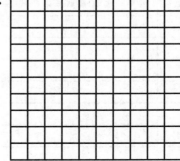

Shaded: _____

Not Shaded: _____

Ways to Write Decimals

Play with a partner.

Materials: one number cube numbered 0–5
one number cube numbered 4–9
one number cube numbered 1–6
one copy of this page for each player

Directions:

Step 1: The first player rolls the number cubes then arranges the cubes in the spaces below to make a decimal number.

Step 2: The player writes that number in standard form, expanded form, and word form.

Step 3: The second player checks to see if the standard form, expanded form, and word form are correct. The first player scores 1 point for each form that is correct. The second player scores 1 point for each form that is incorrect.

Step 4: Switch roles and repeat steps 1–3.

Play 8 rounds.

To make a decimal number, put number cubes here.

Keep your score here.

Score Tally:

You can write your decimal forms in the chart below:

Standard Form	Expanded Form	Word Form

Comparing Decimals

Play with a partner.

Materials: one number cube numbered 0–5
one number cube numbered 4–9
one number cube numbered 1–6

Directions:

Step 1: The first player rolls the number cubes then arranges the cubes in the spaces below to make the greatest decimal possible. The first player then writes the decimal in the chart below.

Step 2: The second player repeats step 1.

Step 3: The players compare their decimals and the player that has written the greater decimal scores a point.

Step 4: Play 11 rounds.

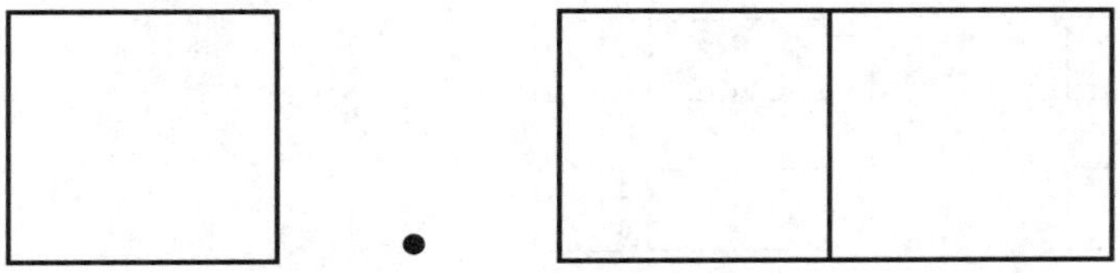

```
┌────────┐      ┌────────┬────────┐
│        │  •   │        │        │
│        │      │        │        │
└────────┘      └────────┴────────┘
```

Write your decimals in this chart:

Player One	Player Two	Who Earns the Point?

Digits and Decimals

1. Write all of the decimals you can make
by placing the digits 1, 2, and 3 in each of the
boxes below. Draw a ring around the greatest
decimal you make. Underline the least
decimal you make. The order of answers will vary.

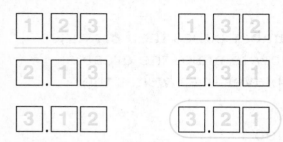

2. Write all of the decimals you can make by
placing the digits 2, 4, and 6 in each of the
boxes below. Draw a ring around the greatest
decimal you make. Underline the least
decimal you make. The order of answers will vary.

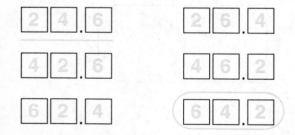

For Exercises 3–10, arrange digits in the boxes to make
number sentences that are true. Use the digits 1, 3, and 5
in each number sentence.

3. $1.00 < \boxed{1}.\boxed{3}\,\boxed{5} < 1.50$

4. $3.00 < \boxed{3}.\boxed{1}\,\boxed{5} < 3.40$

5. $3.10 < \boxed{3}.\boxed{1}\,\boxed{5} < 3.50$

6. $5.00 < \boxed{5}.\boxed{1}\,\boxed{3} < 5.20$

7. $10.0 < \boxed{1}\,\boxed{3}.\boxed{5} < 14.0$

8. $30.0 < \boxed{3}\,\boxed{1}.\boxed{5} < 35.0$

9. $50.0 < \boxed{5}\,\boxed{1}.\boxed{3} < 53.0$

10. $1.50 < \boxed{1}.\boxed{5}\,\boxed{3} < 1.60$

Fractions of a Dollar

Fraction Frank's grocery store is very different. The prices on the things he sells are given as fractions of a dollar. Help these customers find out how much money they owe.

1.

Prices of items:

_____ $0.90, $0.75, $0.50 _____

Total cost: _____ $2.15 _____

2.

Prices of items:

_____ $0.75, $0.70, $0.25 _____

Total cost: _____ $1.70 _____

3.

Prices of items:

_____ $0.30, $0.25, $0.50 _____

Total cost: _____ $1.05 _____

4.

Prices of items:

_____ $0.75, $0.80, $0.90, $0.50 _____

Total cost: _____ $2.95 _____

Decimals and Money

Write the money amount for each. Use a dollar sign and decimal point in each answer.

1. 4 dimes 9 pennies   _____ $0.49 _____

2. 6 dimes 7 pennies   _____ $0.67 _____

3. 1 dimes 3 pennies   _____ $0.13 _____

4. 7 dimes 2 pennies   _____ $0.72 _____

5. 9 dimes 8 pennies   _____ $0.98 _____

6. 5 dimes 0 pennies   _____ $0.50 _____

7. 2 dimes 1 penny   _____ $0.21 _____

8. 4 dimes 4 pennies   _____ $0.44 _____

Write the money amount for each.

9. $\frac{28}{100}$ of a dollar   _____ $0.28 _____

10. $\frac{54}{100}$ of a dollar   _____ $0.54 _____

11. $\frac{1}{100}$ of a dollar   _____ $0.01 _____

12. $\frac{16}{100}$ of a dollar   _____ $0.16 _____

Solve.

13. Alexander has 2 quarters, 3 nickels, and 2 pennies. What fraction of a dollar does he have?

$\frac{67}{100}$ of a dollar

14. Natasha has 4 dimes, 7 nickels, and 16 pennies. What fraction of a dollar does she have?

$\frac{91}{100}$ of a dollar

Name _____

Find the Missing Numbers

Find the missing numbers in each problem. Draw a line from the subtraction problem to the related addition problem.

1.
$$
\begin{array}{r}
0\,.\,7\ 3 \\
-0\,.\,\square\,\square \\
\hline
0\,.\,3\ 5
\end{array}
$$
___0.38___

A.
$$
\begin{array}{r}
0\,.\,\square\,\square \\
+0\,.\,4\ 5 \\
\hline
0\,.\,9\ 1
\end{array}
$$
___0.46___

2.
$$
\begin{array}{r}
0\,.\,8\ 6 \\
-0\,.\,\square\,\square \\
\hline
0\,.\,2\ 7
\end{array}
$$
___0.59___

B.
$$
\begin{array}{r}
0\,.\,\square\,\square \\
+0\,.\,2\ 9 \\
\hline
0\,.\,8\ 0
\end{array}
$$
___0.51___

3.
$$
\begin{array}{r}
0\,.\,9\ 1 \\
-0\,.\,\square\,\square \\
\hline
0\,.\,4\ 5
\end{array}
$$
___0.46___

C.
$$
\begin{array}{r}
0\,.\,\square\,\square \\
+0\,.\,0\ 7 \\
\hline
0\,.\,1\ 6
\end{array}
$$
___0.09___

4.
$$
\begin{array}{r}
0\,.\,5\ 9 \\
-0\,.\,\square\,\square \\
\hline
0\,.\,4\ 5
\end{array}
$$
___0.14___

D.
$$
\begin{array}{r}
0\,.\,\square\,\square \\
+0\,.\,3\ 5 \\
\hline
0\,.\,7\ 3
\end{array}
$$
___0.38___

5.
$$
\begin{array}{r}
0\,.\,8\ 0 \\
-0\,.\,\square\,\square \\
\hline
0\,.\,2\ 9
\end{array}
$$
___0.51___

E.
$$
\begin{array}{r}
0\,.\,\square\,\square \\
+0\,.\,2\ 7 \\
\hline
0\,.\,8\ 6
\end{array}
$$
___0.59___

6.
$$
\begin{array}{r}
0\,.\,1\ 6 \\
-0\,.\,\square\,\square \\
\hline
0\,.\,0\ 7
\end{array}
$$
___0.09___

F.
$$
\begin{array}{r}
0\,.\,\square\,\square \\
+0\,.\,4\ 5 \\
\hline
0\,.\,5\ 9
\end{array}
$$
___0.14___

One Step at a Time

Use the prices below. Write four problems that you would solve by solving a simpler problem. Ask another student to solve your problems. Check students' problems and answers.

1. _____

_____

_____

_____

_____

2. _____

_____

_____

_____

_____

3. _____

_____

_____

_____

_____

4. _____

_____

_____

_____

_____

Multiplication Patterns

You know how to use mental math to multiply any number times 100. Look how you can use mental math to multiply times 99.

Just multiply by 100 and then subtract the original number.

$$\mathbf{8} \times 99 = (8 \times 100) - \mathbf{8}$$
$$\qquad\qquad\downarrow\qquad\qquad\downarrow$$
$$\qquad = \quad 800 \qquad - 8$$
$$\qquad = \quad 792$$

Complete.

1. $7 \times 99 = (7 \times \underline{\quad 100 \quad}) - 7$
$\qquad = 700 - \underline{\quad 7 \quad}$
$\qquad = 693$

2. $4 \times 99 = (4 \times \underline{\quad 100 \quad}) - \underline{\quad 4 \quad}$
$\qquad = 400 - \underline{\quad 4 \quad}$
$\qquad = 396$

3. $5 \times 99 = (\underline{\quad 5 \quad} \times \underline{\quad 100 \quad})$
$\qquad\qquad - \underline{\quad 5 \quad}$
$\qquad = 500 - \underline{\quad 5 \quad}$
$\qquad = \underline{\quad 495 \quad}$

4. $6 \times 99 = (\underline{\quad 6 \quad} \times \underline{\quad 100 \quad})$
$\qquad\qquad - \underline{\quad 6 \quad}$
$\qquad = \underline{\quad 600 \quad} - \underline{\quad 6 \quad}$
$\qquad = \underline{\quad 594 \quad}$

Use mental math to solve.

5. $3 \times 99 = \underline{\quad 297 \quad}$

6. $2 \times 99 = \underline{\quad 198 \quad}$

7. $1 \times 99 = \underline{\quad 99 \quad}$

8. $9 \times 99 = \underline{\quad 891 \quad}$

9. $10 \times 99 = \underline{\quad 990 \quad}$

10. $11 \times 99 = \underline{\quad 1,089 \quad}$

For 11–19, use the answers to Problems 1–9 to help.

$$\mathbf{80} \times 99 = (80 \times 100) - \mathbf{80}$$
$$\qquad\qquad\downarrow\qquad\qquad\downarrow$$
$$\qquad = \quad 8,000 \qquad - 80$$
$$\qquad = \quad 7,920$$

11. $70 \times 99 = \underline{\quad 6,930 \quad}$

12. $40 \times 99 = \underline{\quad 3,960 \quad}$

13. $50 \times 99 = \underline{\quad 4,950 \quad}$

14. $60 \times 99 = \underline{\quad 5,940 \quad}$

15. $30 \times 99 = \underline{\quad 2,970 \quad}$

16. $20 \times 99 = \underline{\quad 1,980 \quad}$

17. $80 \times 99 = \underline{\quad 7,920 \quad}$

18. $90 \times 99 = \underline{\quad 8,910 \quad}$

19. $100 \times 99 = \underline{\quad 9,900 \quad}$

Picture This!

Find each product. Match each digit of the product with the picture in the key. Then find the letter that matches the pictures for the product. Write the letter next to the product. Then find the message.

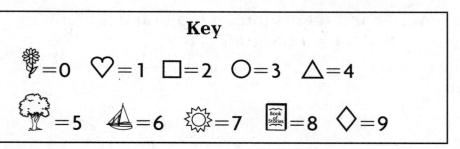

Key

🌼 =0   ♡ =1   □=2   ○=3   △=4

🌳 =5   ⛵=6   ☀=7   📖=8   ◇=9

Example:

$$\begin{array}{r} 27 \\ \times\ 4 \\ \hline 108 \end{array}$$

$108 =$ ♡ 🌼 📖

1. $\begin{array}{r} 65 \\ \times\ 4 \\ \hline 260 \end{array}$ G ____

2. $\begin{array}{r} 36 \\ \times\ 6 \\ \hline 216 \end{array}$ R ____

3. $\begin{array}{r} 47 \\ \times\ 4 \\ \hline 188 \end{array}$ E ____

4. $\begin{array}{r} 52 \\ \times\ 2 \\ \hline 104 \end{array}$ A ____

5. $\begin{array}{r} 32 \\ \times\ 5 \\ \hline 160 \end{array}$ T ____

6. $\begin{array}{r} 48 \\ \times\ 3 \\ \hline 144 \end{array}$ J ____

7. $\begin{array}{r} 21 \\ \times\ 6 \\ \hline 126 \end{array}$ O ____

8. $\begin{array}{r} 28 \\ \times\ 3 \\ \hline 84 \end{array}$ B ____

9. What is the message?

G R E A T

J O B !

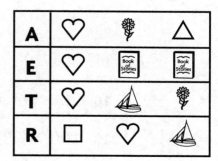

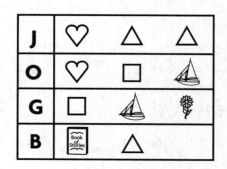

Planning a Picnic

Mrs. Ellis is planning a picnic for 16 people. Use the chart to help her plan the picnic.

Hot dogs	8 in a package
Hot dog buns	4 in a package
Juice	64 ounces in a bottle
Chips	9 servings in a bag
Apples	10 in a bag

1. How many packages of hot dogs would give each person 2 hot dogs?

   4 packages

2. How many packages of hot dog buns would give each person 2 hot dog buns?

   8 packages

3. One bottle of juice will give how many people an 8-ounce serving?

   8 people

4. How many bags of apples would give each person at least one apple?

   2 bags

5. How many bags of chips would give each person at least one serving?

   2 bags

6. How many cookies should Mrs. Ellis bake so that each person can have 3 cookies?

   48 cookies

7. Each picnic table can seat 4 people. How many tables will they need?

   4 tables

8. Mrs. Ellis buys a package of 100 napkins. If each person uses 4 napkins, how many napkins will be left after the picnic?

   36 napkins

Can You Find Me?

Solve the problems below. Then find the answers in the number search. Circle the answers. You will find them upward, downward, diagonally, and backward.

2	2	0	1	4	7	0	5	1	1	0
5	9	5	3	4	6	4	3	7	2	9
7	4	0	0	2	5	8	3	5	3	8
4	3	9	2	0	0	4	1	3	5	6
6	5	1	4	1	5	5	4	1	8	8
2	1	6	4	0	8	1	7	3	1	5
1	1	1	1	4	2	6	9	5	8	0
4	7	4	5	0	4	2	1	1	1	4
1	8	5	3	3	6	8	5	6	2	3
2	0	1	5	8	5	0	8	0	5	1

1. $56 \times 6 =$ ___336___   2. $41 \times 3 =$ ___123___

3. $24 \times 3 =$ ___72___   4. $58 \times 5 =$ ___290___

5. $98 \times 3 =$ ___294___   6. $12 \times 8 =$ ___96___

7. $54 \times 4 =$ ___216___   8. $67 \times 2 =$ ___134___

9. $10 \times 7 =$ ___70___   10. $26 \times 6 =$ ___156___

11. $23 \times 8 =$ ___184___   12. $94 \times 2 =$ ___188___

13. $71 \times 2 =$ ___142___   14. $39 \times 2 =$ ___78___

15. $64 \times 5 =$ ___320___   16. $15 \times 4 =$ ___60___

17. $29 \times 9 =$ ___261___   18. $31 \times 5 =$ ___155___

Sharing Marbles

Cassie, Tony, and Mitchell want to share 26 marbles evenly. They decide to put any extra marbles in a jar.

1. How many marbles will each friend get? _____ 8 marbles _____

2. How many marbles will they put in the jar? _____ 2 marbles _____

Finish this table to show other ways of sharing.

	Number of Marbles	Number of Friends	Marbles for Each Friend	Leftover Marbles
3.	34	4	8	2
4.	29	6	4	5
5.	26	3	8	2
6.	33	6	5	3
7.	15	2	7	1
8.	23	7	3	2
9.	14	4	3	2
10.	22	3	7	1
11.	34	6	5	4

12. A group of 5 friends wants to share a set of stickers evenly. What is the greatest number of stickers that could be left over?

    _____ 4 stickers _____

13. A group of friends shares a batch of cookies evenly. There are 3 cookies left over. What is the least number of friends that could be in the group?

    _____ 4 friends _____

Arranging Digits

Sumi has written 6 different division problems using only the digits 2, 4, and 6. She is wondering which problems will have the greatest and least quotients. Find the quotient for each problem.

1.
```
    2 3
2) 4 6
 - 4 ↓
   0 6
   - 6
     0
```

2.
```
    3 2
2) 6 4
 - 6 ↓
   0 4
   - 4
     0
```

3.
```
      6 r2
4) 2 6
 - 2 4
     2
```

4.
```
    1 5 r2
4) 6 2
 - 4 ↓
   2 2
 - 2 0
     2
```

5.
```
      4 *
6) 2 4
 - 2 4
     0
```

6.
```
      7
6) 4 2
 - 4 2
     0
```

7. Circle the greatest quotient.

8. Draw a star next to the least quotient.

Write your own division problems by arranging the digits 3, 5, and 7 in different ways. Solve each problem.

Check students' problems and solutions.

9.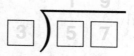

10.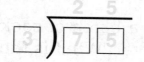

11.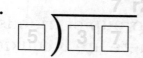

12.

13.

14.

The Division Race

Choose a partner.

Materials: number cube labeled 1–6, game token for each player, paper, and pencil

How to Play: Place game tokens on Start. Take turns rolling the number cube. Use the number rolled as the divisor for the number on your space. Use paper and pencil to divide. Then, move the number of spaces shown in the remainder. If there is no remainder, do not move. The first player to cross the finish line is the winner.

Example: Player's game token is on 86. Player rolls 3. 86 ÷ 3 = 28 r2. Move 2 spaces.

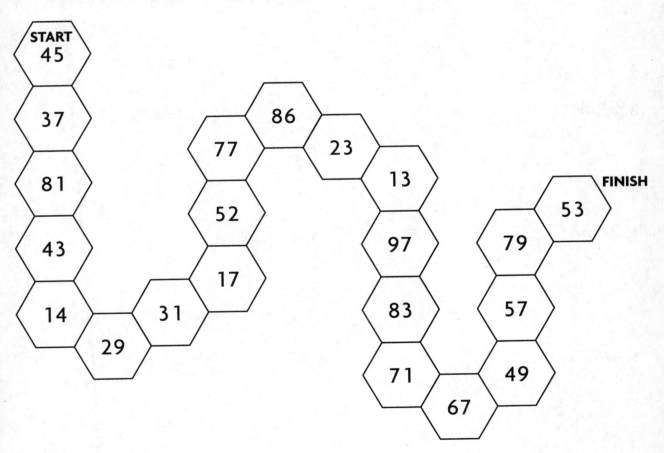

Name _____

Divide and Check

Solve each division problem. Then complete the number sentence that can be used to check the answer. Draw a line from the division problem to the related number sentence.

1. $4\overline{)452}$ $\dfrac{113}{}$

A. ___5___ × 161 = ___805___

2. $5\overline{)805}$ $\dfrac{161}{}$

B. ___2___ × 379 = ___758___

3. $3\overline{)651}$ $\dfrac{217}{}$

C. ___4___ × 113 = 452

4. $2\overline{)758}$ $\dfrac{379}{}$

D. 4 × 118 = ___472___

5. $4\overline{)472}$ $\dfrac{118}{}$

E. ___3___ × 217 = ___651___

Using Estimation

In each exercise, one of the answers is correct. Use estimation to find it. Write the correct answer on the line.

1. $711 \div 9 =$ _____79_____   79   69   59

2. $432 \div 6 =$ _____72_____   82   72   62

3. $360 \div 5 =$ _____72_____   92   82   72

4. $776 \div 8 =$ _____97_____   97   87   77

5. $192 \div 2 =$ _____96_____   96   86   76

6. $220 \div 4 =$ _____55_____   75   55   65

7. $147 \div 3 =$ _____49_____   49   39   29

8. $294 \div 7 =$ _____42_____   52   42   32

9. $472 \div 8 =$ _____59_____   79   69   59

10. $395 \div 5 =$ _____79_____   79   69   59

Challenge CW159